616·85

HUNGRY HELL

HUNGRY HELL

what it's really like to be anorexic: a personal story

Kate Chisholm

✳ SHORT BOOKS

First published in 2002 by
Short Books
15 Highbury Terrace
London N5 1UP

10 9 8 7 6 5 4 3 2 1

Copyright ©
Kate Chisholm 2002

A CIP catalogue record for this book
is available from the British Library.

ISBN 1-904095-23-2

Printed in Great Britain by
Bookmarque Ltd, Croydon, Surrey

To Michael

Contents

Preface

Acknowledgements

Reading

Advice and Treatment

PREFACE

This book is intended as a guide and encouragement for families and friends caring for an anorexic. I know that when I suffered from anorexia nervosa it was almost impossible for those around me to understand why I was making myself so ill. They felt helpless, confused, guilty – and sometimes angry.

Each and every case of anorexia nervosa is different, arising from a peculiar set of circumstances operating on an individual with his or her own unique personality. This is why it is so difficult to treat. One treatment regime may suit 99 patients, but be extremely damaging to patient number 100.

I was in my mid-twenties when I became anorexic, although the seeds were sown in adolescence. But the mental condition is now afflicting younger and younger girls and a rising number of young men. *Hungry Hell* has been written from my own experience of anorexia – that is the only way I can hope to explain it. But I hope that it will suggest what it really feels like to be anorexic.

The dialogues are imaginary; names have been changed where appropriate.

KATE CHISHOLM
April 2002

ACKNOWLEDGEMENTS

These could go on for a while – suffice it to say that I know how much I owe to my family and friends for giving me the courage to go on and the determination to win through. Many nurses and doctors put up with my wayward ways with a patience that I could never muster. I must also thank all those who have helped me in the writing of this book. Never let it be said that an anorexic wins the battle on her own.

1. THE MYSTERY OF FOOD

...The mystery of Food
Increased till I abjured it
Subsisting now like God –
Emily Dickinson, *Collected Poems*

She left home months ago
Somehow we never noticed
That she was going solo.
Philip Gross, *The Wasting Game*

IT'S their thighs and arms I notice first: hip-bones protruding wantonly through thick denim jeans; elbows sticking out painfully from beneath the sleeves of baggy T-shirts. When I look up, their eyes and teeth seem to loom over me, disconcertingly huge; their sickly pale faces distorted by malnutrition. So shocking is their thinness that I find myself rudely staring at them, horrified but fascinated too. How could anyone bear to be so thin?

I am at the Hope Seminar for anorexics at the Bethlem Royal Hospital in south London, and for the first time in more than 20 years I am confronted by what I once was. It makes me want to weep. Not for myself, but for the terrible waste these emaciated bodies represent. Lives dominated not by the need to be slim, but by the inability to eat without terrifying guilt; young girls with so much ahead of them but with their personalities distorted by an obsessive drive to get thin and stay thin.

As they huddle together, whispering among themselves, I am reminded of a flock of exhausted birds, battered by wind and rain after migrating across a limitless ocean. But unlike the birds they will not soon recover their strength to fly on. To get that thin requires going on a long and vicious journey into the innermost psyche; it will take just as long (if not longer) to recover.

It's an odd feeling to realise I was once like them. Even odder not to remember what I looked like at under five stone. And to realise that – despite having once been severely anorexic – I am now as alien to them as they are to me. At a normal nine and a half stone I could never be drawn into their conversation. My 'normal' thoughts about life would seem to them as far removed as if I had come from another planet. The feelings, however, come flooding back. In fact, they never really went away (whenever I shave my legs, I remember the fear of doing that when there is absolutely no fat under the skin so that you feel as if you are scraping at bone).

Which is why I am here. Not to reconnect with that experience – but to exorcise it once and for all by going back to the beginning and trying to understand what made me do it.

**

Becoming anorexic is a last-ditch attempt to do something about the badness, the negativity inside. It's a positive assertion of negation. The anorexic strives to achieve her emaciated form because she perceives that it's the only way she can express what she is feeling. After months and maybe years of being confused and miserable – without finding a way to express it so that others will take notice – she discovers a solution, albeit a perverted one.

She seizes upon what Emily Dickinson once called 'the jouissance of self-starvation' (the American poet knew well the 'inebriation' of hunger), as a way of avoiding all those things that have become too difficult for her: relationships within the family and outside it; the blossoming of her female body; the conflicting voices that continually chatter in her brain, making every decision a nightmare of indecision. As she gets steadily thinner, so she becomes aware that the people around her are at last waking up to how she really feels. She no longer has to pretend that all is well, that she is coping, that she is happy.

By retreating into a life of not-eating, she can both avoid the world outside and be assured of receiving from it the kind of attention that she has been craving. Meanwhile, eating, or rather not-eating, gradually and perniciously takes over her mind, both exhausting her with its obsessive power over all her thoughts and relieving her by the way it drives out all other concerns and anxieties. Life shrinks to hours of worrying about whether or not to eat another half of apple (the staple diet of anorexics: crisp, sharp and crunchy, they exercise the jaw, staving off hunger).

But why choose not to eat? It's such a painful and difficult way to get attention. Is it simply a matter of wanting to be as thin, as beautiful as a willowy supermodel? I don't think so. As Roseanne, a 20-year-old struggling to maintain her healthy weight but still woefully ashamed of her appearance, told us at the seminar, 'I don't know what I was trying to achieve, but it wasn't as simple as wanting to be thin.'

Slimming, dieting, calorie-counting, whatever you choose to call it, is undoubtedly part of the anorexic syndrome, but there is nothing, absolutely nothing, that connects these girls with the kind of 'celebrity anorexia' reported in the tabloid newspapers. Anorexia, of the sort I experienced, and as expressed by the girls at Bethlem, is a crippling, anti-social disease that cuts you off from your real self and everyone you know and love.

It's the exact mirror-image of the designer-label world beloved of *Hello!* and *Vogue* magazines. These girls hate the way they look, not because they don't match up to the fashion babes and movie stars, but because they hate themselves. Not for them the catwalk parade or pouting photo-shoot; rather a retreat into aggressive isolation.

Look around you and you will come across anorexics everywhere – on the Tube, striding down the high street, maybe sweating in the gym. But they will not be seen glamorously made-up, flaunting their female sexiness in micro-dresses and see-through blouses. The girls at the Bethlem had shrouded themselves in baggy trousers, shapeless shirts and huge coats, not just out of shyness and self-hatred, but to keep themselves warm even though it was mid-summer.

The other day a young woman caught my eye as I waited to cross Whitehall. It was the way she was thrusting her paper-thin jaw forward, as if she was doing battle with the world, which made me look at her again. I watched her running across the road to catch a bus and realised that she was anorexic when I saw the way that her trousers were flapping loosely round her thighs. But it was her expression – that pained aggression – which made me certain she was one of us (or perhaps I should say one of what I used to be).

Anorexia nervosa – as it is clinically described – is specifically a loss of appetite brought on by a nervous revulsion, a phobia against food, against mastication and swallowing. The gradual reduction of food intake that characterises the illness may appear to be dieting, but it is much, much more than that.

Many teenagers, confused and disturbed by their changing body shape, are misled into dabbling with dieting by our current belief that beauty lies in thinness, and by the contrary ways that advertising portrays women and food: one moment showing a seductive temptress licking her lips after taking a bite, the next, a mumsy figure stirring the gravy, and the next, a super-thin model eating rabbit food. But most of them will grow out of it as soon as they realise that there are more important things to do in life than worry about what you should or should not eat.

Anorexia may begin by a desire to lose weight, by the thought that if only I were thin – and therefore 'beautiful' – then maybe I would be happy. But the key to understanding its malevolent power is to recognise that not-eating is only the symptom, the outward expression, of an inward *dis*-ease. When an anorexic chooses not to eat, she is making a desperate effort to assert herself. Only desperation would drive someone to deprive herself of so much – not just that extra slice of toast or cube of chocolate, but the whole business of living.

To put on weight is frightening not because the anorexic feels it is going to make her less attractive but precisely the opposite. She fears that another pound or two will bring back her womanly curves (or, in the case of very young anorexics, allow them to develop in the first place) and force her to take on the adult world: being responsible for herself, and open to desires of all kinds.

Rather than slimming to be beautiful, the anorexic sheds her pounds as a denial of her femininity. She does not wish to make herself available to life; or rather, she fears what the consequences of becoming available will be, of what will happen if she allows her true personality to emerge.

It is not a slimmers' disease – not really. And you will rarely see anorexics preening themselves in front of the mirror, admiring their increasingly lean outline. Mirrors are the Enemy, to be avoided, not stared into – as any anorexic will tell you. To look into a mirror is to look into yourself, with all your flaws.

One of the telling symptoms of anorexia is the distortion in body-image, so that you believe yourself to be hugely fat when in fact you are skeletal. But although this is true – you do always feel huge and lumpen – deep down you know that your legs, thighs, ankles, arms, wrists, fingers are all painfully thin. When I was in hospital, I was once asked by a research student to draw the outline of my body as I saw it. It was supposed to show how different the reality was from what I imagined. But I knew what my shape really was, and hated both its bony thinness and my feelings of hugeness. It *is* possible to hold two contradictory thoughts in your head at the same time: that is the paradox of anorexia. (There are no photographs of me from that time. I was just too horrified by what I looked like – even though I had created myself in that image.)

***

At first, the not-eating is deceptively unobtrusive; often unseen, unnoticed, unobserved – even by the anorexic herself. It begins through a perverse, unconscious decision – as if the subconscious, rigidly suppressed for so long out of fear that you might otherwise stop being the person others want you to be (or whom you think others want you to be), suddenly says 'Enough' and takes control of the conscious mind.

In my case I do still remember shreds of a conversation in my room in our university flat in Edinburgh. It must have been 1974. I'd never heard of anorexia – no one had – until that grey, wintry afternoon. We were drinking coffee, chatting inconsequentially, kept in by the weather on a boring weekend. Friends had called round, along with a couple of girls I did not know and do not now recall, except that one of them had red hair. She began to tell us about the sister of a friend who was suffering from anorexia and how terrible it was. Something in what she said resonated with me. And although at the time I was showing no signs of the illness (except that my periods had stopped while I was studying for my A-levels) and had lost no significant weight (and would not do so for some time to come), it was as if deep down I recognised that this was what was wrong with me.

Did I consciously choose to become anorexic that afternoon? Could I willingly have seized on a solution that I had heard would lead me into such a relentlessly miserable and ultimately horrifying way of life? No one really knows. Anorexia provokes and shocks because it seems so inexplicable. To feel guilty about eating cream cakes and chocolate appears reasonable (or is it?) but to stop eating altogether suggests insanity.

The trouble is that once you get used to eating less it seems easier to carry on reducing until the whole business of eating becomes meaningless. Most people will have experienced at some time that feeling of not wanting to eat – whether it be before an exam or important interview, on falling in love, or after bereavement. The intensity of emotion created by anxiety, romance or grief takes away the appetite, the ability to recognise that one is hungry. Everything tastes like cardboard and swallowing becomes difficult.

Usually, this phase soon passes; the appetite begins to respond again to the light-headedness and stomach pangs of hunger; the taste buds regain their sensitivity; eating becomes desirable, if not immediately enjoyable. With the anorexic, however, something goes wrong with the hunger/appetite equation so that she will complain constantly, even when obviously in dire need of food, 'But I'm not hungry.'

Perhaps puberty and all the confusion that comes with it – both physical, as hormonal activity triggers actual changes to the body, and mental, as the protective veils of childhood innocence and perspicacious self-confidence suddenly fall away – creates in some teenagers an existential burden. What's the point of all this business of eating and defecating if it only brings death at the end of it?

I began not-eating simply by eating less. At the time, I thought it was about becoming fitter, more energetic and more positive about my time in Edinburgh. Looking back with hindsight, I can see now that I had been miserable for years; that going to university had been a massive disappointment. I was terrified of walking into the lecture halls filled with as many as 300 students; terrified of making a fool of myself in the library, which was huge, modern and open-plan (no ivory towers there); and terrified of going to parties in case someone asked me out, in which case I had no idea how to behave since I was terrified of doing something (or even witnessing something) of which my parents would disapprove.

By my second year I had begun to restrict how much I was eating and to run everywhere. I got a kick out of it, and enjoyed feeling my bottom and breasts getting flatter and flatter – for years my rib-cage always stuck out more than my breasts. It was a relief to become more and more androgynous. I had my hair cut short in a boyish crop (this was the early 1970s, so everyone else had floppy hair and was wearing Laura Ashley smocks under those smelly goatskin coats from Afghanistan). The fact my periods had stopped never bothered me and I had no idea what it felt like to 'fancy' anyone. I would observe my friends who had been resolutely without a boyfriend, for a while getting hornier until there came a point (usually a Saturday-night party) when the arrival of a new man on the scene became inevitable. It seemed like a totally foreign experience to me. What was I supposed to do if some unsuspecting male did take an interest in me? I hadn't a clue, and was too scared of my ignorance and naivety being exposed to talk about it to any-one.

I took comfort in not-eating. It gave me a sense of

power over my destiny. I was not going to sacrifice myself on the altar of men and sexuality (this was, after all, the era of free love and hippie excess). I would survive as an individual by ensuring that my mind controlled my body, rather than vice versa. No one was ever going to see me being soppy over a man.

I suppose at this stage it would be true to say that I was eating less and less from a wish to be slimmer, more attractive, more like Twiggy, that stick-thin icon of the late 1960s (an entirely misplaced ambition since I've never had cheekbones and am too short to have shapely thighs). My problems did begin with a dislike of my bodily shape; with the belief that if I were thinner, then perhaps I would be more like my friends, who *appeared* to be at ease with themselves and with boys. And yet they were, in the end, much more to do with the way I felt about myself; with my grinding sense of hopelessness about what I could, or would, become.

***

It has been said, cryptically, that a slimmer wants to be a size 8 whereas an anorexic wants to be size 0;

like an alcoholic, the anorexic begins in control but ends up not knowing when to stop. There is some truth in this. Strange things happen to the mind after it has been deprived of nutrition for many months, if not years. And some would argue that, as in alcoholism, anorexics have a physical predisposition to the illness. Food deprivation sets off in some people a series of chemical changes that cause loss of appetite and reluctance to eat.

This is an explanation that many families would love to hear, avoiding as it does that horrid business of self-analysis. But it's too simple. Looking back, I can see that I was predisposed to anorexia – hypersensitive, perfectionist, fearful and yet also fiercely driven by the need to prove myself. I also grew up in the 'typical' anorexic family: earnest, close-knit and restrained emotionally. And yet my younger sister bears no sign of the illness. So why did I fall victim?

As a child I hated being physically sick; don't we all? But with me it preyed on my mind, haunted my dreams, made me ever afterwards averse to carrot rounds and Brussels sprouts. I was not just hypersensitive; I placed all my fears about the world on to food. If I eat this, I will be sick. I must be greedy; that's why I'm ill. At the same time I was always in the kitchen helping my mother (I was the elder daughter of five children) or poring over recipe books. This was the 1960s when, despite the small number of those who were Swinging, Sunday mornings were still devoted to church not shopping, followed by lunch at one with roast beef and all the trimmings, the biggest feast of the week. At Brownies we were awarded badges for ironing (I failed mine), while at Guides we learnt first aid and how to use face-powder. I craved a pair of Pretty Polly 'American tan' stockings worn with a frilly (and hip-pinching) suspender-belt, while at the same time being disgusted (and crippled with pain) when my periods began.

Deep down I understood that growing up, becoming a woman, would involve nurturing, feeding, providing, and I was very ambivalent about this. I would spend hours making endless trays of biscuits, scone rounds, iced cakes, to prove myself as a dutiful daughter and accomplished 'woman', while at the same time wishing I could break free of my feelings of obligation to my family and knowing somehow that I was different. This, at least, is how I explain it now. At the time, it expressed itself in endless arguments with my fathe͏ hero-worshipped and felt antago because I felt that we always had to worse, since he was a vicar, what God – wanted.

I had become uneasy about being a vicar's daughter. At first I had really enjoyed the marks of respect and special attention that we were given as the children of the vicarage. I was proud of my Dad and loved to hear him in church. But once the awful self-consciousness of adolescence had set in, I began to hate walking up through the church to sit in the vicarage pew at the front. And I suppose I felt odd about my father's role as priest one minute and father the next. People would call at all hours, wanting banns-of-marriage forms, passports signed, money, exorcisms, confessions, emotional counselling. I was once woken up in the middle of the night by the persistent ringing of the doorbell (I was alone in the house at the time while the rest of the family were away on summer holiday). A group of Armenians, one of whom was terrified that he was about to be murdered, was at the door wanting protection. We felt part of Dad's job – and responsible even for his pastoral work.

This was difficult enough for an awkward teen-ager, but especially so once I began to question the mysterious business of the Bread and Wine and its translation into the Body and Blood of Christ. I wanted to believe in it, because not to do so felt like a betrayal of Mum and Dad, and yet intellectually I knew that it didn't make sense to me. That I didn't become anorexic much earlier is perhaps more of a mystery than the fact that I became anorexic at all.

Guilt. That's the crucifying element. Guilt for eating too much (in my pre-anorexic days I enjoyed puddings, cakes, chocolate in that naughty, but nice way); guilt for not thinking the same way as everyone else; guilt for wanting to lead a different life than was possible in the net-curtained, cherry-tree avenues of suburbia, especially as a vicar's daughter with a heightened sense of responsibility towards her mother.

And I suppose the danger signal was that I never talked about any of this to anyone. As Philip Gross explains in *The Wasting Game*, a series of poems written from the viewpoint of the father of an anorexic daughter: 'She left home months ago,/Somehow we never noticed/She was going solo.'

***

Lunch at the Hope Seminar was a miserable affair.

The usual trays of sandwiches had been supplemented thoughtfully by mounds of diced raw vegetables and bowls of fruit, but all the anorexics still crept away into corners with hardly anything heaped on to their paper plates. Shy and hesitant, when they did speak out, their voices were soft and diffident, as if to say anything about how they felt was a tremendous effort. And yet a certain defiance and inner energy seemed to emanate from them. Never be taken in by the retiring, modest manner of anorexics; these girls have hearts and minds of steel.

As the Italian psychiatrist Mara Selvini Palazzoli wrote in *Self-Starvation*, her revelatory book on anorexia as an expression of family dysfunction, 'The body is our meeting place with others, and its rejection is at one and the same time a rejection of sociability, human solidarity and responsibility.'

By not-eating, anorexics are expressing their unwillingness to engage with the world; they are shunning the unpleasant business of living and dying. In an ideal world, an anorexic would like never to eat as proof of her superiority and inner resourcefulness. While being emotionally very needy, she perversely attempts to prove that she has no need of any sustenance – either emotional or physical – but can exist entirely without.

Anorexia nervosa as it expresses itself in aggressive not-eating can hardly be claimed as a 'holy' act, but in order to understand how and why it can take such pernicious hold of the personality we need to seek out its philosophical roots. Fasting practices are embedded in most religions; denial of the flesh making possible, it is believed, true meditation on the Divine. The medieval female saints in the Christian world, for example, starved for God. St Catherine of Siena reputedly ate nothing but the odd bean and used an olive twig to make herself sick before she took Communion so that she would not defile the Body and Blood of Christ by having profane 'viands' in her stomach. She died in 1380, believing to the end that by fasting she was doing God's will.

Catherine was revered for her spirituality – not something associated with the anorexic girls of today. On the contrary, they are regarded as the most difficult of patients because of their defiant self-will and devious behaviour. Those sharp-edged, unsmiling faces have none of the beatific tranquillity of a saint; and food rather than God fills their minds. There is, however, a touch of the ascetic Christian Father about many of them. After all, they, too, are striving for the total suppression of all bodily desires, and have taken themselves off into an emotional desert to prove their self-reliance.

When I studied monastic history at university, I was enthralled by the tales I read of women achieving an almost superhuman disregard for pain and hunger, living holed up in tiny cells, refusing all food except bread and water, devoting themselves to achieving a state of closer communion with God – and thereby proving that they were superior to their more worldly male brothers in Christ. They were attractive to me because they were able to dispense with boyfriends, sex and marriage. I naively imagined that they had found a way to be true to themselves without bowing to what was expected of them. And I was often tempted by the idea of becoming a nun. What held me back was the fear that the religious life would deny me the freedom to think for myself; that I would have to devote myself to God and to become a 'bride of Christ', literally wearing a wedding ring to show this. Hidden deep, very deep, within anorexics is a desperately strong desire for life – and all its pleasures; where else would they derive the strength to deny all its blandishments?

Reading Karen Armstrong's autobiography,

Beginning the World, I was not surprised to discover that she became anorexic after leaving the convent in Oxfordshire where she had lived for seven years under the rigorous Rule of St Ignatius Loyola. She had been drawn to the religious life as a 17-year-old because it enforced a total suppression of the body and its temptations (in the Loyolan orders at that time, they even practised flagellation). But once back in the world she could no longer hide from the inner demons that the convent wall had protected her from.

A man asks her out for dinner at an Italian restaurant, and she is unable (or unwilling) to find an excuse:

The lobster leered pinkly and evilly at me from the white plate, smothered in a violent terracotta sauce. I felt a sprinkling of sweat erupt on my face, which had suddenly gone cold.

'I told you,' I smiled pleadingly across the tiny table for two, 'I just can't eat this.'

Robin smiled back, bland but determined.

'But I say you can...'

Robin lifted a slab of shell-like flesh to his lips. A drop of sauce was left on his thin, lower lip and I watched his tongue flicker out to retrieve it...

'It's such a waste of money!' I protested, thinking of the alarming sum on the menu. It was a sum that would have kept me in food for three months.

'Nonsense.' Robin addressed himself to the lobster again. 'You'll eat it, if we sit here all night.' I watched him, mesmerised as he dug his fork into the strong-smelling gunge again, conscious of the light tinkle of conversation from the other tables, the ripple of civilised laughter.

'It's absolute rubbish to say you can't eat,' Robin continued, his mouth full and a strand of lettuce just visible, clinging to the side of his mouth. 'It's pure masochism and self-indulgence…'

Karen not only had to learn how to manage, aged 24, on the lean budget of a university student − a good excuse not to eat − but also how to deal with the utter confusion of being suddenly let loose in the world of the post-Pill Swinging Sixties. She descended into anorexia because it was a way out: she was back in the world, but she was still not really part of it because she had not yet learnt how to deal with it.

The terror that Karen felt when faced by her plate of lobster was not just distaste for its bloated decadence and horror at its digestive connotations (the lobster was perhaps rather too drastic a transition from her usual Ryvita and cottage cheese). She knew that by taking one mouthful she was entering into an exchange with Robin. She was right: the evening turned sour; expectations had been raised. But her reaction was heightened by the way that, for her, food had become associated not with the mere function of survival but with her emotional inability to adjust to the world in which she found herself.

Every anorexic can describe similar moments of pure terror when faced with a plate of perfectly innocuous food. And this is what those around them can never understand. After all, to eat is to live; we all have to do it. How can you possibly not want to eat?

What Karen discovers is that anorexia is far more powerful than religious belief. It's an all-consuming passion. It requires constant vigilance to ensure that hunger is never satisfied, nor thirst assuaged. When 'every bite becomes a major guilt-arousing decision', as one anorexic has described her experience, there is very little room left in the mind for thoughts of God or anything else.

It is incredibly difficult for those who have never suffered from anorexia to appreciate the depths of feeling aroused by the process of eating in the mind of the anorexic: the horror of indulging oneself; the fear that one day you will just go on and on eating until bursting-point; the blind panic which dries up the saliva and constricts the throat; the nightmare that one day you will be overcome by the urge even to eat the dogshit in the gutter as you rush along with your eyes downcast, unable to look upwards and engage with the world around you.

Psychiatrists from Freud onwards have explored the ways in which an anorexic's response to her instinctive need for food has been perverted. Perhaps something went wrong in her initial bonding with her mother; perhaps the mother did not react positively and correctly to the signals that her baby was giving her; perhaps those first sensations of feeding, of oral satisfaction, were blighted by the mother's incomprehension of her baby's needs or her inability to meet them.

Some, maybe all, of these things may be true. But such explanations are of little help to the anorexic as she struggles to eat even a morsel of toast, scraped ever so thinly with low-fat margarine. Or to the mother who is helplessly watching her beloved child slowly and deliberately fading away. The tragedy of anorexia is the way it draws all those around you into its tortuous, cruel web. Not only is the anorexic herself trapped in a tormenting cycle of not-eating; her family and friends, too, become enmeshed in a world where food is the only thing that matters.

**

Boredom, a sense of isolation, an obscure feeling of helplessness and uselessness, of having no part to play in what happens to you – a gradual lessening of your enthusiasm for life – these are the signs. And when these feelings are combined with an uneasiness about food, then the conditions are set for anorexia nervosa to develop. Whether or not it does so depends on whether the potential sufferer experiences some kind of life crisis.

Mine occurred as I arrived at teacher-training college knowing that it wasn't what I wanted to do. I had spent the year after leaving university working as a shop assistant and in a children's home while applying for jobs that required a degree – with absolutely no success. I knew that I was making a mistake; but I felt that teaching was the only thing I could do: everyone expected it, especially the college. Deep down, very deep, I knew that I wanted to write books, but I had not the courage to go for it. And in any case how did one begin?

I had been reducing my eating for years without really noticing it, other than the pleasure I got out of denying myself. But it was not until I was faced with the need to find a life for myself, and the realisation that I had left university with none of my social problems resolved (my longing to be like everyone else and to have a boyfriend, but my fear of what this might mean) that I plummeted in weight. With the skewed logic peculiar to anorexics, I sought the magical weight of four stone and six pounds, believing that at that weight I was safe from all life's pressures (I seem to remember I had weighed that when I was four-foot six, just before puberty).

Gradually, imperceptibly, I had become indifferent to food, just as I believed life had become indifferent to me. As I struggled to survive a day of teaching practice on a bowl of porridge for breakfast and an apple for lunch, so my understanding of what life could offer me shrank away to nothing. All I wanted was to retreat. For if I did not teach, what then was left for me to do? Meanwhile, I had discovered the intoxication of not-eating. Better than drink or sex – or so I believed then.

2. DRUNK WITH STARVATION

It is as if your nerves were strung tight. Like violin strings.
Anything: lovely words, or the sound of a concertina from
the street: even a badly played piano can make one cry.
Not with hunger or sadness. No!
But with the extraordinary beauty of life.
'Hunger', Jean Rhys

To hunger is to overcome the pull of gravity, and to
liberate the spirit from the prison of its flesh.
Simone Weil

The summer of 1976 was brilliantly hot. When at last London returned to normal after six weeks of being like the Mediterranean, I went off to Winchester to learn how to be a teacher. We paid for all those sunshiny days in an autumn of relentless rain, with only the odd buttery-gold afternoon of fine weather. It was a bumper year for berries and conkers. I bought an OS map and walked for miles up and over the hills around the cathedral city, with a new sense of power now that my body was pounds lighter and my mind sharper from lack of food. Hunger – the real kind, provoked by prolonged food deprivation – induces a thrilling, endorphinous high.

Jean Rhys understood this all too well. She became an actress after arriving in London from the Caribbean island of Dominica in 1907, but she could never get used to the chilly drabness of England; nor was she ever a success on the stage. Her life appears to have veered wildly from extravagant luxury to absolute penury – mostly the latter. Her short story 'Hunger' tells of five days in Paris after the female narrator has been abandoned by her lover and finds herself with no money and no job. In just four pages Rhys describes – with the careless yet bracing economy of her novels – the five degrees of self-inflicted starvation. She was not, as far as I know, anorexic, but she perceived acutely its peculiar states of mind.

She had experienced how you begin by wanting food intensely, but gradually feel more and more cleansed as the body empties itself, freeing the mind so that it floats above you, detached from all worldly concerns.

Starvation – or rather semi-starvation – coffee in the morning, bread at midday, is exactly like everything else. It has its compensations. but they do not come at once...

To begin with it is a frankly awful business…

On the second day you have a bad headache. You feel pugnacious. You argue all day with an invisible and sceptical listener…

On the third day one feels sick; on the fourth one starts crying very easily… A bad habit that; it sticks.

On the fifth day…

You awaken with a feeling of detachment; you are calm and godlike. It is to attain to that state that religious people fast.

Lying in bed, my arm over my eyes, I despise, utterly, my futile struggles of the last two years. What on earth have I been making such a fuss about? What does it matter, anyway?…

Oh! the relief of letting go: tumbling comfortably into the abyss…

Not such a terrible place after all. One day, no doubt, one will grow used to it. Lots of jolly people here…

No more effort…

It is as if your nerves were strung tight. Like violin strings. Anything: lovely words, or the sound of a concertina from the street: even a badly played piano can make one cry. Not with hunger or sadness. No!

But with the extraordinary beauty of life.

Actually, I don't remember very much about the highs; the lows take precedence in my memory of those years of continual, nagging hunger. But there were times of exultation – like the bitterly cold winter's afternoon I spent in Guildford, Christmas shopping with an old friend from school. I was freezing cold, but can vividly recall the blue of the high-pressure sky and the smell of the frost as it ate into my bones. Even in the midst of my descent into breakdown, I could feel more alive than ever before. There were moments of fierce insight, of a kind that I had never experienced as an undergraduate. It was as if my brain was unclogged by not having all that heavy food to process. I seemed to need less and less sleep and could walk further and further each day. I disdained company; not just because I no longer felt able to compete on its terms, but also because it no longer seemed necessary to me.

Not-eating is a powerful weapon; it detaches you from the world. You no longer have to meet with people, or share with them a social life. By not turning up for meals in college, I could avoid the men who were beginning to show an interest in me. Now that I was thinner – and apparently in control – I had a new-found confidence in my body, which, ironically, meant that I felt I was at last being noticed by the opposite sex as, deep down, I had always wanted. I began to feel that I might just enjoy being attracted to, and attractive to, men. And perhaps that's what tipped me over the edge, because as soon as someone began to take a real interest in me, and I felt some kind of response, I ran away, almost literally, after having coffee with him and realising that he wanted more than just a cup of coffee – and so did I.

At night, driven half-mad with hunger, I would roam Winchester in search of somewhere to buy something suitable to eat – an apple or one of those small packets of peanuts and raisins. Not even a packet of crisps was allowed – far too indulgent. I was living on the edge, 'high' on the feeling that my body, and its capricious desires, was at last under control.

Or so I thought. I deluded myself into believing that I could exist on the tiny amount that I had decided was OK, slowly reducing the number of Ryvitas I was allowed each day but never abandoning the apple for lunch or the half-packet of minestrone soup (always the same flavour) for supper. I was in triumphant mode. Well, at least for part of the time. At others, I was desperate. Desperately cold, desperately tired, desperately hungry – and desperately scared. Even if I had wanted to eat, by then I no longer could.

The Norwegian writer Knut Hamsun wrote a novel about hunger. His hero, whose name you never learn, is an egotistical writer who disdains to get a job because of his determination to write a great book; a series of almost deliberate misfortunes means that he never has the money to buy food. Strictly speaking, *Hunger* is not about anorexic excess, but it describes with acute precision the driving forces that lead a person to starve amidst plenty.

I knew about this novel for years but was too scared to read it, sensing that it would be too uncomfortable an explanation of my own uncompromising behaviour. It is. *Hunger* was written in 1890, more than 50 years before Camus's *L'Etranger*, but it prefigures that novel's ruthless depiction of a man's essential solitariness. Hamsun's hero takes to wandering the streets of Kristiania, 'that strange city which no one leaves before it has set its mark upon him', to keep at bay his desire for food:

> Here I was marching around so hungry that my intestines were squirming inside me like snakes, and I had no guarantee there would be something in the way of food later in the day either. And as time went on I was getting more and more hollowed out, spiritually and physically, and I stooped to less and less honourable actions every

day… Rotten patches were beginning to appear in my inner being, black spongy growths that were spreading more and more…

'Rotten patches', 'black spongy growths'. No wonder I had been too scared to read this novel. Too scared to recognise the corrosive effects on the mind of prolonged and self-induced starvation. You should never underestimate the brutality of the anorexic personality. It is the darkness inside that gives the anorexic the willpower she needs to deny herself so much.

The other side of that darkness is the delirium, the ecstasy of egotistical control. And Hamsun's hero veers between the two as he descends into semi-starvation:

I was drunk with starvation, my hunger had made me intoxicated … I suffered no pain, my hunger had taken the edge off; instead I felt pleasantly empty, untouched by everything around me and happy to be unseen by all… There wasn't a cloud in my mind, nor did I feel any discomfort, and I hadn't a single unfulfilled desire or craving as far as my thoughts could reach. I lay with open eyes in a state of utter absence from myself, and felt deliciously out of it.

Like alcoholic intoxication, hunger and its highs can become addictive. As the body gets used to receiving less and less food, so the highs become more difficult to attain, requiring increasingly rigorous feats of denial and over-exercise. It is also like alcoholism in being utterly self-absorbed and selfish. You become incapable of seeing anyone else's point of view.

Hunger holds you like a vice; never letting you go, cutting off all lines of communication. Not-eating becomes a manic, quasi-religious experience; an act of self-purification. I began to equate eating with defilement. So that anyone who suggested that perhaps I would feel better if I ate a little more was actually asking me to defile that hard-sought purity. Just as they had always failed to understand how I felt and instead sought to control me (or at least that is how I experienced it, and that is all that matters), now they were asking me to give up the one thing that made me feel I was at last in control of myself and my destiny.

Simone Weil, the French philosopher, began starving herself when she was a teenager in the 1920s. Looking back on how she felt at 14, she wrote to a friend: 'I fell into one of those fits of bottomless despair that come with adolescence, and I seriously thought of dying because of the mediocrity of my natural faculties. The extraordinary gifts of my brother, who had a childhood and a youth comparable to Pascal's, brought my own inferiority home to me.'

She was actually just as 'extraordinary', if not more so, as her brilliant mathematician brother André. But she never believed this herself, refusing either to eat enough or to make anything of her dark, vibrant beauty. She deprived herself of all comforts (except cigarettes) because she lived always with a deep sense of her own unworthiness. At the same time she was also a keenly driven person, pushing herself not just to outdo others in her rigorous search for knowledge – for the truth of existence – but also in the punishing way she treated her body, living on less and less food, and attempting, despite her soft-skinned, intellectual upbringing, to earn her living as a manual worker in a car factory.

The desire to outdo everyone else, to be the thinnest, eat the least amount, walk the furthest, suffer the most is very much part of the anorexic make-up. Even now when reading books about anorexia, I notice that I feel superior if I discover that the sufferer has not gone down to such a low weight as I did. Maybe this is merely an unattractive aspect of my personality. Maybe. But the determination required of an anorexic is part and parcel of her fierce ambition, not necessarily for material success but for recognition of her intellectual and spiritual superiority.

By depriving herself of food, Weil – just like the early 19th-century Romantic poets, starving in their garrets, not from poverty but from an ascetic devotion to their art and an abhorrence of down-to-earth reality – was seeking to remove herself from all earthly temptation. 'To hunger', she said, 'is to overcome the pull of gravity, and to liberate the spirit from the prison of its flesh.'

I miss that intensity of experience, the sensation of being totally in control of my body and my mind; until, that is, the inevitable collapse. The thrilling power and energy created by the release of those panic-stricken endorphins – desperate to ensure that the body keeps running even when on empty – cannot be denied. Deluded by this unnatural energy, you are certain that what you are doing is the only thing you can do – not-eating is an expression of your true personality, your specialness and individuality. Anyone who tries to convince you otherwise is attempting to thwart the very essence of your being.

In a sense, anorexia takes you back into early childhood, to the time as a toddler when you first gained mastery over your physical body and began to recognise your own power as a person; when all the world revolved around you and your concerns. To be anorexic is to be totally out of touch with the impact of your behaviour on others; and to be as demanding of them as a frustrated child. Whatever you are doing – or feeling – becomes of paramount importance. It cannot be altered by what others around you may think or say.

But this is not to say that you *are* a child. To exercise that much control, experience that degree of despair, you will need to have developed more of your cognitive abilities; to be emerging, just, into adulthood. A report in the *Sunday Times* based on research carried out at the Royal Hospital for Sick Children in Glasgow suggested recently that anorexia can begin in children as young as three. This is giving too much significance to the food fads of toddlers emerging from babyhood and beginning to assert their individuality by not eating what has been prepared for them. For parents, and/or doctors to categorise such young children as anorexic – and to treat them accordingly – is surely inappropriate, if not dangerous, locking them into a cycle of behaviour that they would otherwise pass through as a growing phase.

The awful, deceiving paradox of anorexia is that, although it leads inexorably to breakdown of some kind, along the way it gives you a life-enhancing sense of mastery over who you are and an incredible physical energy. I used to go on marathon walks, seeing everything around me with exceptional clarity. At the same time, I was losing touch with those closest to me, unable to communicate what I was feeling or to care about what was happening to them. Hunger – both the addictive highs, when I felt supremely confident of my ability to survive on nothing, and the obsessive lows, when my body craved sustenance – was beginning to take over my mind.

Leonard Woolf complained of his novelist wife, Virginia: 'It was extraordinarily difficult ever to get her to eat enough to keep her strong and well. Superficially, I suppose it might have been said that she had a (quite unnecessary) fear of becoming fat; but there was something deeper than that, in the back of her mind or in the pit of her stomach – a taboo against eating.'

Taboos against eating have become much more common (Virginia Woolf was born in 1882 and died in 1941) now that we are overfed and faced by so much choice. According to the Eating Disorders Association, one in 60 people (1.15 million) in the UK will experience either anorexia, bulimia or compulsive eating at some time in their life. Many more will experiment with the multitude of diets suggested in magazines and books while watching obsessively the endless programmes about food and cooking on television. No wonder we are all in such a muddle, extolling the virtues of thinness while being bombarded by images of indulgence.

For the anorexic, not-eating is much more than a mere taboo against eating. It's a cry for help. *I would eat if I could but I can't.* In my case, I was scarcely aware of what was happening at the time – except that I felt that I was being taken over by something which I could not have explained or described to anyone. All I knew then was that I liked the way my body felt, and believed that by getting thinner and thinner I would like it more and more. Part of me knew that I was being perverse; that rather than facing up to myself I was running away. But the exhilaration of being in control of my hated body was a much more powerful force within me than the consciousness that something was going wrong, seriously wrong.

As I weighed myself yet once more, thrilled that I had lost another couple of pounds, I was also perturbed by my not-eating ways. I knew deep down that this could not go on for ever. But I had no idea why it was happening, and no idea how to stop it. It was as if I was being taken over by something outwith myself. I was losing touch with the person I had been. Despair had found its panacea – in starvation.

3. FORTRESS ANOREXIA

Perfectionist, Stubborn, Overconscientious, Neat,
Meticulous, Parsimonious.
Personality profile of an anorexic

The young anorexic was caught in a cruel trap. She
refused to eat in order to preserve her personal identity,
but in order to preserve her life she simply had to eat,
and this she experienced as an act of self-betrayal.
Mara Selvini Palazzoli, *Self-Starvation*

Just before the anorexic collapses – as inevitably she must – she will be at her most untouchable, secure in her belief that, unlike all those around her, she can survive on less and less food, that she has her not-eating under control. She will be quite unaware that she is seriously underweight, and, while refusing to eat in the fear of what ingesting food might do to her body, she may well indulge herself by taking excessive amounts of laxatives.

Fortunately for me, I hated the bodily processes so much that I was never tempted either to force myself to vomit or to play around with pills. It's probably what saved me. Not so the singer Karen

Carpenter, who died of heart failure in 1983 after playing the dangerous game of using diuretics, which drain the body of its essential minerals. To the end, she apparently remained oblivious to the fact that she was committing slow suicide. I didn't ever think I was damaging myself. Safe in my cocoon of not-eating, I believed that I was not thin enough to die, nor had I any idea that by refusing to nourish myself I was endangering my health.

The most serious consequences of prolonged anorexia in the young are bone-thinning (osteoporosis) and infertility (an anorexic's father told me that his daughter was so shocked when she was warned that being anorexic would stop her having children that she began to eat). Anorexics who begin not-eating when very young will not mature, develop breasts, or grow to their full height. Those who persist in extreme not-eating will destroy their digestive systems and weaken all their organs.

Strange things begin happening to your body after the loss of 25 per cent of your body weight. Your periods stop; soft, downy hair (lanugo) grows on your arms and thighs (so I'm told; this never happened to me); and your pulse becomes very slow so that you use up less energy despite being hyperactive and constantly on guard, never relaxing even for a moment. The body adjusts, shutting down all inessential functions (that's why menstruation ceases). The circulation reduces, so that hands and feet remain permanently cold and often become reddened. The heart rate slows and the blood pressure falls. Heart failure is a threat, but usually only at very low weights and when purgatives are being used, which destroy the body's inner balance as well as damaging the digestive organs and oesophagus. That's what makes anorexia so dangerous: you can go on for years eating a very limited diet without noticeable damage, except that it cuts you off from living and the potential of being your real self, while drawing all those around you into your despairing, not-eating thought-world.

The body will recover quickly as soon as normal eating begins again, but the mind takes much longer, sometimes years, to regain its equilibrium. In his explanation of anorexia nervosa on the website of the Priory Hospital in south-west London, Dr Peter Rowan says that: 'Subsequent return to normal weight and eating pattern is usually accompanied by the restoration of physical normality, including the ability to have children.' But he adds, 'The return to normal eating unmasks the underlying psychological issues...' And to lead a 'normal' life again will take much longer; it is, says Dr Rowan, 'a task that may be slow and tentative as a result of the profound loss of confidence that is so characteristic of the illness'.

***

'Mum. *Stop going on at me. I'm* NOT *hungry.* NOT *hungry.*'

'*I was only suggesting you might feel better if you ate something.*'

'*But I don't want anything.*'

'*You only had an apple for lunch. Surely you can manage just a little piece of pie.*'

'*No, I can't. Please don't make me. Really, I can't.*'

'*Well, you're never going to get better if you don't try.*'

'*But I'm not hungry. Really, I'm not hungry.*'

'*Even if you're not hungry, you should try to eat just a little something.*'

'*But I don't want to. I'm not hungry. I'm really not hungry.*'

'*Why won't you eat, just like everyone else, darling?*'

'It's not like that. I'm just not hungry.'

'But you must be.'

'No. I'm not. Anyway, what's the point? I don't want any food. I'm not hungry.'

'Well, I'll just put a little on a tray and you can have it upstairs in your room. You don't need to eat it with us.'

The girl takes the tray and retreats to her room, muttering.

'She doesn't understand. I can't eat all that. It'll make me huge. Anyway, I'm not hungry. I'm really not hungry. I just can't eat it. I can't. I'm not hungry. NOT hungry. It'll make me fat. My stomach's so huge. I don't want to eat it. I'm not hungry. Really, I'm NOT hungry. I'll get fat. She just doesn't understand. I can't eat it. My stomach's huge. I'll get fat. I'm just not hungry…'

***

Just as all physical feeling is suppressed, so all emotion drifts away, leaving the anorexic devoid of any sensations but extreme fear. I can still recall vividly that absence of feeling. I was so detached from the girl I had been, from all the things that had made me the person I was, that it was as if that girl had never existed. I had lost touch with myself because my memories no longer had any relevance for me. Looking through photos of myself when younger was like looking at pictures of a stranger. Time had slipped out of focus so that the past was as if it had never existed; the future, meanwhile, loomed ahead of me frighteningly. What was I going to do with it? Where could I find a job? I no longer wanted to see my friends because I had nothing to say to them, and anyway I didn't want to eat. I felt as if I didn't fit in anywhere. Not at home with my family. Not out with my friends. Not anywhere.

At the time I felt as if I was trapped in an endless tunnel that was pitch-black with never a glimmer of light. But, looking back, I can see that it was as if I had sealed myself up in an impregnable fortress. I was unreachable, totally cut off, and absolutely convinced that no one could help me.

The crunch came after six weeks' of teaching practice. It was not very dramatic. I just couldn't face going back to college after the Christmas vacation. Eating had become such a struggle that I no longer ate meals with my family, surviving on just apples and cheese. I was freezing cold all the time, could not sleep, and felt as if I had no inner strength.

Day after day, my diary records, 'CAN'T EAT! CAN'T EAT!' But I had no idea what was wrong with me. A 'Showdown with Ma and Pa' occurs, but I have no memory of it. No doubt they were trying to find out why I wouldn't eat. But I really had no idea. 'Stomach seems to be permanently closed up', I note in my diary, and 'Have to see doctor – can't face any-one – can't talk about it without weeping – awful.' But I recorded nothing of what was going on inside my head. On Boxing Day 1976, I confess that 'I am awfully worried over eating because no improve-ment and it is making me feel so ill.'

My parents must have been desperately worried, but I, of course, have no memory of that. In the end, I was 'rescued' when a friend of the family who had once been anorexic came for dinner and recognised at once what was wrong with me. She suggested to my parents that they should try to get an appoint-ment for me with the specialist, Dr Peter Dally of the Westminster Hospital, who had cured her. My GP was most reluctant to refer me, believing that I could get better myself – with a bit of effort and some vitamin pills. And at the time, it is true, I was not dangerously low in weight. But my parents must have insisted because my diary shows that I was seen within a week.

By then I had deteriorated not just in weight but, more disturbingly, in my ability to cope, crying at the least thing and yet also bristling antagonistically whenever anyone suggested anything that might help me to feel better. When I look back on that winter, all I see is myself, scared of everything and totally alone. I was in a place where no one could reach me, no matter how they tried. For my family it must have been very different: cut off from me, their once-happy daughter, and yet totally embroiled.

***

'Please, darling. You must eat something today. You had nothing yesterday, except an apple and a piece of toast and an apple and a piece of toast the day before. If you don't eat, you'll never have the energy to look for a job.'

'Shut up. Shut up. SHUT UP. If I eat anything else, I'll feel bad.'

'But can't you do it, just this once, just for me?'

'Why? It won't make any difference. I don't need anything. Anyway I'm OK. Just leave me alone. There's no point in me eating. I'm fat enough already. Look at me. Look at my fat tummy.'

'But you're just skin and bone. Don't you remember how pretty you used to be?'

'No, I don't. And anyway I wasn't pretty. I was fat.'

'No you weren't. But what's the use? You never listen to me.'

'But I do. I just don't want anything to eat. I can't. I just can't. Please don't make me.'

'No one's forcing you to do anything, darling. But surely a little bit of pasta won't hurt?'

'But I don't want anything. Anyway, what's the point? I'm no use at anything.'

'But that's nonsense, darling. You've got a really good degree – and you're a brilliant cook.'

'No I'm not. And in any case cooking won't make me a fortune. No one cares these days whether you can cook or not. I'm no good at anything that will get me a job.'

'But of course you are, darling. That's silly talk. Why don't you eat a bit more. Then you'll feel better.'

'Please Mum. Just leave me alone. I'll never find a job. I just know I won't. I told you, I'm no good. I'm just no good.'

***

Feminist writers have often asserted that just as Victorian oppression resulted in fasting girls and later the Suffragette hunger strikers, so anorexics today are 'heroic freedom fighters' whose struggle is against male greed and the oppression of women. The psychotherapist Susie Orbach (whose first book on the subject, *Fat Is a Feminist Issue*, was published in 1978) has written that anorexia is 'a dramatic expression of the internal compromise wrought by Western women... in their attempt to negotiate their passions and desires in a time of extraordinary confusion'.

No doubt the anorexic's flight from self and sanity is partly exacerbated by finding herself in a world where the roles of men and women have become so muddled. Women are supposed to be either domestic heroes running their families with supreme efficiency and dashing glamour or super-successful career-girls, competing with their male colleagues for the top job. They are encouraged to be promiscuous, but are then vilified for being so. Men, meanwhile, have to be both caring and competitive, complementing the domestic goddess while being threatened by the career-girl.

But any mother, father, friend, boyfriend, doctor, nurse who has had to cope with an anorexic will know that at heart the illness is about a very personal, private and selfish retreat from everything that the world represents. What is so horrifying is the constant denial that is expressed in every gesture: the angular, starving body; the weak, bleating voice; the stooped, I-am-not-here posture.

***

'How about coming shopping? I want to find something to wear for the party. Maybe we could go and have a coffee somewhere afterwards?'

'Oh, I don't think so. I feel so tired.'

'But I haven't seen you for ages. We've got such a lot to catch up on.'

'I don't know. I haven't been anywhere. I haven't got anything to tell you. Anyway, won't your boyfriend want to go shopping with you?'

'Oh no. He's hopeless. Hasn't a clue. And never says what he likes. Anyway I want to see you. I want to know how you are.'

'Oh, I'm OK.'

'Well, if you really don't want to come shopping

with me, why don't you come round this evening? We're going to hire a video. You needn't eat with us, if you're worried about that. We'll probably get a takeaway anyway.'

'I don't think so. Sorry.'

'But I thought it might do you good.'

'Thanks anyway.'

'Well, if you're sure…'

'I'm just not in the mood for a film.'

'So are you going to go to the party?'

'I haven't thought about it.'

'But you must come. It will be such fun to meet up with everyone again.'

'Oh I don't know. I'm not sure whether to go or not. I'll probably be too tired.'

'Well, if you don't come to the party, we must get together anyway. Maybe we could all go out for a pizza or something?'

'Oh I don't think so… What's the point? I've got nothing to talk about.'

'But we want to see you.'

'No one's going to want to see me like this. Anyway, I really don't feel like it. There's no point. I've nothing to say.'

***

In her book, *The Golden Cage*, the American psychiatrist Hilde Bruch describes, from her experience of working with anorexics, what it feels like to be anorexic:

> On first encounter anorexics who absolutely refuse any suggestion to eat and relax give the impression of great stamina, pride, and stubbornness. This impression is replaced, on closer contact, by the picture of underlying ineffectiveness, inability to make decisions, and constant fear of not being respected or rated highly enough. These youngsters appear to have no conviction of their own inner substance and value, and are preoccupied with satisfying the image others have of them. The whole childhood of the anorexic is infused by the need to outguess others and to do what they think the others expect her to do.

There is absolutely nothing 'heroic' about anorexia. As Mara Selvini Palazzoli says of her patients: 'These solitary little girls are full of fears: fear of life in general; fear of scholastic failure; fear of falling short of all sorts of expectations; and fear of doing the wrong thing. In short they have an apparently inexplicable and obscure feeling of fatal impotence, of a total lack of control over their lives.'

This 'lack of control' is experienced by the anorexic as a total absence or loss of self. One of the things that goes wrong inside the anorexic mind is that she loses all sense of who she is, and with this all ability to recognise or understand what she is feeling. This is perhaps the key to the psychiatric disorder. It is as if she is suffering from a kind of emotional dyslexia. She will be unable to identify or know what her feelings are, so that each time they come along she will have to learn again, painfully, the appropriate response.

Hilde Bruch explains this further. She believes that for a child to mature appropriately she needs appropriate levels of encouragement. Where these are not enough (or, more significantly, are perceived by the potential anorexic to be not enough), then maturation fails to occur. The anorexic will have no sense of herself as an independent, sensate being, and will not develop the cognitive abilities of an adult. She will lack the maturity to think in abstract, formal terms or to evaluate situations independently, without emotion.

The impact of this as she moves from childhood into adolescence is that she will not fully understand the adult world in which she finds herself. She will misread the relationship between her parents, will be confused by the sexual relations that she sees her friends embarking on, and will begin to lose ground at school where until now she will probably have been a star pupil. The disparity between her intellectual and emotional development will result in a bewildering distortion. She will not see the world clearly; everything will appear blurred and confusing. A frightening loss of confidence will follow. If these bad feelings are then transferred on to food, what may have begun as dieting will end in anorexia.

***

'When did you first stop eating?'

'I don't know. Anyway I haven't stopped eating. I just don't want all that meat and cake and fattening stuff. I would eat it if I could. But I just can't face it.'

'So *why* can't you face eating? Everyone else does.'

'I don't know. I just can't. I feel full up all the time. I wish I could eat. That's why I'm here, isn't it?'

'Well, yes. We want to help you. To get you to eat like everyone else.'

'But I'll never be able to do that. I just know I won't.'

'But why not? You're like everyone else, after all.'

'No, I'm not. I'm not like anyone else. I've made such a mess of things.'

'What do you mean, you've made a mess of things?'

'I don't know. I just have.'

'In what way.'

'I'm just so useless. There's nothing I can do.'

'Well, maybe not at the moment. But when you're better.'

'But I'll never be better.'

'That depends on you.'

'What do you mean?'

'Well, if you started to eat more.'

'But how can I do that? I'm eating such a lot as it is.'

'Well, you won't put on weight unless you start eating those extra snacks.'

'But I don't want to put on any more weight. I'm fat enough already. I just can't eat any more.'

'That's up to you. If you really want to get better...'

'I do want to get better. I just wish I could eat. But I can't. I can't live with myself if I eat all that stuff.'

'It's up to you. You know that. You're an intelligent girl. You know that only you can choose whether or not to get better.'

'But I can't. I'm useless. And anyway it's not up to me. You're supposed to be helping me, aren't you?'

**

So what are the vital signs of anorexia nervosa? How can an anxious mother know whether her daughter is sliding into the illness or is merely dabbling with slimming? Much has been written about the deceitful behaviour: the hiding of half-eaten sandwiches and soggy Weetabixes under the bed, behind the sofa, in the dog's basket; the avoidance of meals and assertions 'Oh, I've already eaten' (we all do it, even those of us who succumb long after our teenage years are past). But such childishness only begins *after* the battle with food has been fought and lost.

Hilde Bruch gives three criteria which she believes are the key factors leading up to anorexia:

• a disturbance in how the anorexic sees her body so that

she is quite unaware of her severe emaciation, believing that her thinness is quite normal;

• a loss in the ability to perceive and identify body stimuli, not just hunger but also fatigue (and including an absence of sexual feeling);

• and a paralysing, overwhelming sense of ineffectiveness which pervades her every thought and activity, so that she feels that all her actions are merely responses to the demands of others.

The disturbance in body image does happen. It begins with a permanent abdominal discomfort, as if your stomach is always swollen, but grows into a belief that no matter how thin you are it cannot be thin enough. Once anorexia had taken hold of me, I did know that my extreme thinness made me different from everyone else – but that was what I wanted to be, aloof and untouchable. I lived in a world without feeling – or rather my feelings were so jumbled up that I existed in a permanent state of confusion.

The outward signs of potential anorexia are: amenorrhea; a gradual retreat from socialising with friends her own age, especially when the opposite sex is involved; an increasing anxiety about performing well at school (I used to be told off for spending too long on my homework), together with dissatisfaction with her appearance. Always restless and pretending never to be tired, she will insist on walking miles rather than taking the train or bus. More significantly, she will display a persistently negative reaction to what is going on around her. Nothing will please her; and in her view, no one will care about her. And yet she will be over-zealous in her concern for others, and in her desire to see them eat while she increasingly denies herself even the smallest indulgence. As an increasing number of foods are eliminated from her diet – potatoes, pasta, pastry, meat, butter, sugar – so the anorexic will fall ever deeper into the illness.

Whether or not she will continue on this down-ward spiral depends very much on what happens next in her life. Many potential anorexics are saved from serious illness by going away to college and discovering their independence (or changing to a school that better suits their personality), or finding a companion who really understands them, or mak-ing a career choice that brings some kind of person-al fulfilment. The interplay of personality, family setting, life chances is complex and unfathomable. But unless something comes along that puts an end to the continual battle going on inside the anorexic between her many selves, arguing ceaselessly about whether she should or should not eat, whether she should take part in life or resist its every allure, then the anorexia will take hold and the girl you once knew will disappear behind a wall of not-eating.

4. FASTING GIRLS

I do not remember that I did ever in all my Practice see
one, that was conversant with the living so much
wasted with the greatest degree of a Consumption
(like a skeleton only clad with skin).
Richard Morton, *Phthisiologia*, 1694

Fasting women and girls have made more noise in
the world than fasting men.
Charles Dickens, *All the Year Round*, 1869

There's nothing new about fasting girls. Look hard
enough and you will find them always, in some guise
or other, defiantly asserting their alienation and dis-
concerting the physicians of their day. And, from the
beginning, their symptoms have remained the same:
extreme fasting, extreme withdrawal, extreme resistance to treatment.

What is shocking about anorexia today is not
that it's on the increase; in fact, according to the
most recent Department of Health statistics, the
number of anorexic patients seen by a consultant
actually went down slightly, year on year, in the ten
years between 1989 and 1999. No, what is shocking

is that the illness has been around for centuries and yet even now so little appears to be understood about how to treat it.

Anorexia nervosa does have the highest mortality rate of any psychiatric condition – up to 20 per cent of patients will die. The recovery rate is also very low: only 33 per cent of those considered to be full-blown anorexics will recover completely (whatever that might mean). Even though I did begin to eat again, and to live what appeared to be a normal life, I was so demoralised by the negative view of the illness given me by the medical establishment that I never believed I could get really better. And until recently I was never able to say the word 'anorexic', let alone read anything about the illness.

This was not just because of my unwillingness to recall how I had allowed myself to break down so completely that I was content to live for months on end in a hospital ward doling out tea to the other patients and stitching endlessly a patchwork quilt that was never made whole. On the contrary, I spent years trying to work out for myself what all those years of not-eating had been about. But I always felt that the way the illness was being portrayed in the popular press and on television had nothing to do with how I experienced it. And I assumed that since no one I met during my years of treatment had ever been able to explain anything to me, there would be no point in seeking out medical textbooks on the condition.

And yet anorexia has always been present, and the way it presents is always the same. Even in the late 17th century doctors were writing down tellingly detailed accounts of their anorexic patients. To read them now is to be astonished that anyone could so acutely describe the illness, let alone so many years ago. I found it immensely reassuring: maybe I had not been such a freak after all? But it is also deeply disturbing. If so much has always been known about the illness, why does the medical establishment still appear to be so flummoxed when faced with a not-eating teenager?

'The Pathogonomick Signs, or those which do evidently manifest the beginning of this Consumption, are a decrease of the Patient's Strength, and a loss of Appetite, without any remarkable Fever, Cough, or Shortness of Breath,' writes Richard Morton in his *Phthisiologia; or, A Treatise of Consumptions* (translated in 1694 from the original Latin edition of 1689). 'At first it flatters and deceives the Patient, for which reason it happens for the most part that the Physician is consulted too late.' Morton details two case-histories – one female (who ultimately dies) and one male (who recovers 'in great Measure'):

Mr Duke's Daughter in St Mary Axe in the year 1684 and the Eighteenth Year of her Age, in the month of July fell into a total suppression of her monthly courses from a multitude of Cares and Passions of Her Mind, but without any Symptom of the Green Sickness following upon it. From which time her Appetite began to abate, and her Digestion to be bad; her flesh also began to be flaccid and loose, and her looks pale… she was wont by her studying at Night, and continual poring upon Books, to expose her self both Day and Night to the injuries of the Air, which was at that time extreamly cold… The Spring following, by the Prescription of some Emetick, she took a Vomit… from that time, loathing all sorts of medicaments, she wholly neglected the care of her self for two full Years… I do not remember that I did ever in all my Practice see one, that was conversant with the living so much wasted with the greatest degree of a Consumption (like a skeleton only clad with skin)…

All the classic symptoms are here – amenorrhoea, ardent overwork, fanaticism about fresh air and exercise, a reluctance to accept treatment, even purging and vomiting. And this in a society without cameras, wall-to-wall mirrors and books on dieting; in which beauty was thought of in Rubenesque proportions: big bosoms, fleshy arms and enormous thighs. Here was proof that anorexia has little to do with our image-conscious times. It has always been present – and the way it presents is always the same. There is no way that it is 'catching', an hysterical reaction by feeble womanhood to contemporary media representations of what the ideal woman should be. It represents something much deeper – and more unsettling.

There was an epidemic of fasting in the late 17th century. Twenty years before Morton's *Phthisiologia*, John Reynolds published an account of the year-long fast of the 'Derbyshire Damosell', Martha Taylor, in his *A Discourse Upon Prodigious Abstinence*. Reynolds wrote his pamphlet for the recently established Royal Society and he was less concerned to give a description of an illness than to prove that Martha's 'achievement', if it could be so-called, was no miracle, ordained by God, but was possible physiologically. (As scientific explanations began to supersede the supernatural, it was no longer acceptable to believe that fasting had saintly overtones.) Buried within his convoluted pseudoscientific arguments is the detail that Martha was 'emaciated thereby unto the ghastliness of a skeleton... *her belly slap'd to her back-bone* [my italics], so that it may be felt through her intestines'.

When the philosopher Thomas Hobbes was staying at Chatsworth as a guest of the Devonshires in 1688, he was taken to visit another of the Derbyshire Damosells, who claimed to have eaten and drunk nothing for six months, except 'to wet her lips with a feather dipt in water'. She had been accorded 'heavenly status' by her local priest (Reynolds's pamphlet was intended to dispute such miraculous nonsense). Hobbes was not taken in. He declared in a letter to a friend that she was 'manifestly sick', adding that '*part of her belly touches her back-bone*' (my italics).

Note the detail. Three centuries later, when the American feminist Naomi Wolf went to the doctor suffering from anorexia as a schoolgirl in the 1970s, she was told by him, according to her book *The Beauty Myth*, that he could feel her spine through her stomach.

Anorexia has always been present; and the way it presents is always the same.

Another epidemic of fasting girls appears to have broken out in the late Victorian period. The feminists love this: Victorian bourgeois patriarchy oppresses women leading to a rise in anorexia. But that's far too simplistic. The parents of Sarah Jacob of Llethernoyadduccha in Wales, whom Dickens writes about in his 1869 essay 'Fasting Girls' (which he published in his magazine *All the Year Round*), were anything but bourgeois. They were, however, allegedly cashing in on their daughter's ability to survive without food by using her as a freak show, 'an exhibition for curiosity-hunting visitors', rather like the hunger artist in Kafka's celebrated short story.

Dickens quotes from the report of the 'district medical officer' who was sent from London to investigate whether her claims were fraudulent. 'The girl's face was plump,' says the physician, 'her cheeks and lips of a rosy colour, her eyes bright and sparkling, and her muscular development very inconsistent with such (alleged) wonderful abstinence from food.' He had been prevented 'by excuses and expostulations on the part of the parents' from examining the girl's back, which he says 'would have told something to him as a medical man concerning the presence or absence of gastronomic action'. But he concludes, nevertheless, that the parents 'honestly believed' that their daughter was surviving on nothing; it was the girl who was being deceitful. His reasons: 'The construction of the bed and the surrounding old Welsh cupboards and drawers in the room were all favourable to the concealment of food.'

The girl, he says, had deluded her parents, and was suffering from hysteria – almost as common a diagnosis in Victorian medicine as our own unidentifiable viruses. When the royal physician Sir William Withey Gull first published his reports about the patients who were turning up at his London clinic suffering from wilful malnutrition, he referred to them as hysterics. But he soon realised that this was inaccurate; males, too, could be afflicted: 'That mental states may destroy appetite is notorious, and it will be admitted that young women at the ages named (ie 16–23) are specially obnoxious to mental perversity. We might call the state "hysterical"… I prefer, however, the more general term "nervosa", since the disease occurs in males as well as females.'

But even then he was reluctant to lose the designation 'hysterical', and when in 1873 he gave a lecture about the illness to the Clinical Society of London he called it, 'Anorexia Nervosa (Apepsia Hysterica, Anorexia Hysterica)'. Gull advised that the patients 'should be fed at regular intervals, and surrounded by persons who would have moral control over them; relations and friends being generally the worst attendants'.

A haunting page of engravings accompanies the published version of his talk. Three of his patients – referred to as Miss A, Miss B and Miss C – are shown in profile both before treatment and after recovery. Misses A and B appear docile, subdued, their heads bent, their expressions melancholy, in both the 'before' and 'after' portraits. Miss C, however, in her 'before' picture, holds her head erect, her emaciated face shrieking an almost triumphant defiance: 'I will survive'. In her 'after' portrait, she is unrecognisable: her head downturned, her face bloated, her expression blank.

Anorexia has always been present, and the way it presents is always the same – and so is the reaction it provokes.

'Woe to the physician who, misunderstanding the peril, treats as a fancy without object or duration an obstinacy which he hopes to vanquish by medicines, friendly advice, or by the still more defective resource, intimidation,' warned Charles Lasègue, who was treating anorexics at the Hôpital de la Salpetrière in Paris in the 1860s and 1870s, at the same time as Gull was publishing his reports. 'With hysterical subjects,' he explains, 'a first medical fault is never reparable. Ever on the watch for judgments concerning themselves, especially such as are approved by the family, they never pardon; and considering that hostilities have been commenced against them, they attribute to themselves the right of employing these with implacable tenacity.'

When I read this, I recognised immediately my own experience of the illness. It was a revelation. I had spent years blaming myself for being such an awkward and unresponsive patient. Now I can see that hostilities break out on *both* sides – and are characteristic of the condition, not specific to the patient.

Anorexia nervosa, writes Lasègue over 100 years ago, is 'constant enough in its symptoms to allow of physicians who have met with it controlling the accuracy of the description, and to prevent those who have yet to meet with it in their practice being taken unawares'. It *has* always been present, and the way it presents *has* always been the same.

Lasègue describes with acute precision the various stages that the anorexic will go through as the illness takes hold of her (or him). Any parent or carer reading his article 'On Hysterical Anorexia' (published in English in the *Medical Times* of 1873) will not only recognise everything he says as being true of their anorexic child or partner but also feel comforted by the knowledge that here at last is someone who at least appears to understand what is going on.

At first, says Lasègue, there will be 'uneasiness after food, vague sensations of fullness...

> The patient thinks to herself that the best remedy for this indefinite and painful uneasiness will be to diminish her food... Gradually she reduces her food, furnishing pretexts sometimes in a headache, sometimes in temporary distaste, and sometimes in the fear of a recurrence of pain after eating... Meal after meal is discontinued... and almost always some article of diet is successively repressed, whether this be bread, meat, or certain vegetables – sometimes one alimentary substance being replaced by another for which an exclusive predilection may be manifested for weeks together.

The fear of food becomes so great that it is only possible to accept one kind at a time: an apple, a carrot, a slice of toast or scrambled egg. To diverge from this rigid adherence to the same foods is to wander into unexplored, wild territory. Lasègue was intrigued (not infuriated) by one patient – a young woman who lived a long way from Paris – who insisted on eating only a particular kind of biscuit made by a Parisian baker; nothing else would do. Another would only eat raw rhubarb.

'At this point, the disease is declared,' he says, and 'the anorexia will have taken over the patient.' She will believe that 'I cannot eat because I suffer', although quite what she means by her suffering no one will be able to discern. The loss of weight may not be all that obvious and, since the reduction in food has been so gradual, the body will have adapted to surviving on less so that the patient is probably hyperactive. 'So far from muscular power being diminished,' says Lasègue, 'this abstinence tends to increase the aptitude for movement. The patient feels more light and active.'

Eventually, however, the anorexic's appearance and stubborn behaviour will provoke a reaction from her family and friends. Once this happens, then the 'mental perversion' of anorexia begins to express itself. The patient 'disdainfully tastes the new viands, and after having shown her willingness, holds herself absolved from any obligation to do more. She is besought, as a favour, and as a sovereign proof of affection, to consent to add even an additional mouthful to what she has taken; but this excess of insistence begets an excess of resistance.'

Every anorexic will recognise in that description her own agony on being faced with a plateful (or even a mouthful) of food, knowing that it is impossible to eat it, despite the pleadings of those whom you love. 'Love', in any case, is as foreign to an anorexic as greed, lust and sloth (although she will be no stranger to pride, anger and envy).

'The anorexia,' says Lasègue, 'gradually becomes the sole object of preoccupation and conversation. The patient thus gets surrounded by a kind of atmosphere, from which there is no escape during the entire day...' By this stage, not only the anorexic but also her whole family will be involved in her battle with food. She will not have given up on food entirely: 'The patient willingly joins her family at meals, on the condition that she is allowed to take only what she wishes.' Provided that she is allowed to continue eating just as little she pleases, peace will reign; any attempt to contravene this – either by her family, or by her own natural instinct for survival, desperate for some energy-boosting nutrition – will provoke an explosion; a childish temper tantrum.

'I do not suffer and must then be well' replaces 'I cannot eat because I suffer' as her explanation for her loss of appetite. This may go on for months until the body is weakened to such an extent that some kind of physical collapse occurs. (My knees suddenly refused to support me, so that I found myself unable to step up on to the Tube.) 'For the first time,' says Lasègue, 'her self-satisfied indifference receives a shock.' This is the moment, he says, when 'the physician should resume his authority'. To intervene earlier, with an unreceptive patient, will only reinforce her resistance. But at the point when she is forced to face up to the reality of her own weakness, the physician will find that, 'Treatment is no longer submitted to with a more passive condescendence, but is sought for with an eagerness that the patient still tries to conceal.' She will 'submit with a semi-docility, with the evident hope that she will avert the peril without renouncing her ideas and perhaps the interest that her malady has inspired'. But she *will* submit.

At last, a voice of common sense and realism. Lasègue even admits that in treating these patients, 'I have passed through repeated perplexities'. And that he knows patients who 'ten years after the origin of the affection have not yet recovered the *aptitude* for eating like other people'. As a general rule, 'we must look forward to a change for the better only taking place slowly – by successive starts'.

When I read this in the hallowed silence of the Wellcome Library reading room, I kept muttering out loud to myself, 'Yes, yes, yes.' This *is* exactly what it feels like. Lasègue's insights are startling because they are so rarely to be found in the literature about anorexia (despite the reams that have been written), and yet there they have been in print for over a hundred years for anyone to read.

Anorexia has always been present, and the way it presents is always the same – and so is the reaction it provokes: hostility and misunderstanding.

5. TOO CLOSE TO THE BONE

The mind is its own place, and in it self
Can make a Heav'n of Hell, a Hell of Heav'n
Milton, *Paradise Lost*

O the mind, mind has mountains; cliffs of fall
Frightful, sheer, no-man-fathomed.
Gerard Manley Hopkins, 'No worst, there is none'

Perspicacious Sylvia. Well, you always were, while
apparently only Little-Miss-I-Am-Not-Here-At-All.
Doris Lessing, *The Sweetest Dream*

I put on my perky pink beret as I left the flat, just
in case I needed to remind myself who Kate
Chisholm now is. Wispy grey clouds scudded across
a pale turquoise sky, chasing away the sun; a chill
wind nipped at my cheeks.

As I walked up the steps to what was once All
Saints (the psychiatric wing of the Westminster
Hospital), I realised that it was 25 years almost to
the day since I had first seen its High Victorian insti-
tutional walls. What would it feel like to revisit
Canny Ryall Ward, the room in which I spent two

months in 1977, drugged, stuffed with calories, and told I must be either a lesbian or possessed by the Devil?

The room looks so light. And so narrow. How, I wondered, had they fitted 16, or was it 18, beds in here? And why do I think of it as having been so dark; no sunshine, no fresh air, and absolutely no sense of the parkland beyond its many windows. Now the room is painted white and lined with desks and filing cabinets in its new incarnation as the photographic archive of the Imperial War Museum. Three of its walls are broken up by those tall, thin windows you see in paintings of Victorian schoolrooms. Even with drab hospital curtains and fading paintwork, the room must surely have sometimes been filled with light during those short wintry days.

The corridor which led to the toilets is still there. I can see now that it's actually a bridge to the adjoining wing and its walls and ceiling are made of glass. More light then, which has been wiped totally from my memory. But I do remember being chased down that corridor by a zealous nurse wielding a teaspoon laden with marmalade; marmalade that I had ever so carefully scraped off my breakfast toast and which she had ever so carefully scraped off the plate and on to a spoon.

The patient is put to bed at the start of the treatment and told that she must stay there until she has regained a definite weight... Bed rest [a treatment regime whereby we were kept in bed and not allowed to stand up, not even to go to the toilet, until the required weight had been reached – I suppose it was to prevent us burning up precious calories] is at first total and no visitors are permitted... Chlorpromazine [a powerful sedative] is given by mouth... As much as 1,600mg a day has been needed in a difficult case. It is essential to increase the dose until the patient's resistance to eating is overcome; at the same time her sense of panic at the sight of food and post-prandial discomfort diminishes. Modified insulin therapy is also begun at once, starting with 10 units each morning one hour after breakfast and progressively increasing the dose until the patient sweats and becomes drowsy. Interruption then takes place with a large meal...

So wrote Dr Peter Dally in 1969. A consultant psychiatrist at the Westminster, Dally had become a leading expert on anorexia nervosa because of the success of his treatment regime with young teenage girls. It was pioneering work; and I was deemed fortunate to have been accepted as one of his patients.

On his ward at All Saints, his aim was to increase

the calorific intake of his patients from a 'light diet' of just 1,500 calories to 5,000 calories in a fortnight. In other words, in just 14 days from entering hospital, his dangerously underweight patients, who for weeks, if not months, had been eating little more than a few crackers and an apple each day, were (as I recall) expected to consume:

For breakfast:
Cornflakes with milk and sugar
Two eggs, scrambled
Two slices of white toast with butter and marmalade

For morning snack:
Complan
Two slices of white toast with butter and marmalade

For lunch:
Meat or fish
Two scoops of potato
Vegetable
Pudding with custard

For afternoon snack:
Complan
Two slices of white toast with butter and marmalade

For supper:
Meat or fish
Two scoops of potato
Vegetable
Pudding with custard

For bedtime snack:
Complan
Two slices of white toast with butter and marmalade

'In this way,' says Dally (referring to the 'gradual' increase in calorific intake), 'abdominal discomfort, which can be unpleasant and frightening at the start of treatment, is minimised. The patient's confidence is gained and reassurance is constantly given; the attitude initially should be a firm, decisive one. Little attempt to uncover psychological problems is made until the patient's weight increases to near normal, when drugs are reduced in dosage or stopped.'

So far as 'abdominal discomfort' is concerned, certainly I don't remember pain. But then, of course, I was on drugs and was soon on anti-depressants as well – the old-fashioned kind that left you with a persistent, cloying dryness and terrible metallic taste in your mouth. But I do recall the sight of my bloated stomach, stretched like a balloon that was about to burst. There was a constant buzzing sensation in my head, I lost all ability to concentrate (even to read the Mills & Boons that were given to me), and my legs were always hot and tingly, as if too much blood was constantly being pumped round my body.

I had in no way been hostile to Dr Dally's suggestion that I should come into hospital for treatment. On the contrary, I was extraordinarily relieved that at last someone was going to help me. Not that I understood what that help could or would be. I was quite unaware that my problem was my resistance to eating. I knew that I could not eat, and I knew that something was wrong, but I thought it had much more to do with my inability to cope and my realisation that I did not want to teach.

I walked into All Saints, aged 24 years and four months, naively believing that once I was there I would be cured straightaway; and that in its protective environment I would be able to eat – just like that. When I asked how long I would be in hospital, I was told, 'Oh, about three weeks.' I was appalled; I had never known anyone spend longer than a week inside. I soon discovered that most of the other patients on the ward had been there for at least a couple of months. Why so long?

On arrival, I did eat – my first meal. I remember the astonishment of the nurses who watched over me as I ploughed through the fish and chips with bright green peas (it was a Friday) without a murmur. Maybe I was that rare thing: a co-operative anorexic. Or not really one at all? Such illusions did not last – on either side. I couldn't understand why we needed to have a rigid set of rules and incentives to persuade us to eat. Because we were not allowed to get up, even to go to the toilet, we had to use bed-pans. We also had imposed on us a Reward and Punishment programme, which meant that we had to reach certain weight targets before we were allowed to get up, have a bath, wash our hair, see our visitors (who were sometimes turned away if we had failed to put on that extra ounce), or go for a walk. For the system to work, we had to be weighed each and every morning, first thing while it was still dark (it was part of the night nurses' duties – they also gave us our breakfast before the other patients were awake).

I took all the drugs without questioning anyone, but became increasingly confused. What was happening to me? Before coming into hospital, I had been finding it hard to function properly as an independent grown-up, but now I truly felt I was cracking up. I was unable to think straight or keep in touch with the person I had once been. I didn't want to talk to anyone about my feelings, my past, my fears, hopes, dreams and failures, least of all to nurses and doctors whom I had never met before. This was partly because I had no idea what I was feeling, and so really did have nothing to say, but mostly because I regarded all attempts to 'analyse' me, to determine my personality, as being like a game of cat-and-mouse: how could I avoid saying what they wanted me to say? More to the point, I very soon realised that, by giving over to the staff at All Saints all responsibility for what I ate, I was going to have to put on weight – and fast – which I really did not want to do. The war about food had begun.

Twenty years later, Dally co-wrote another book – *Understanding Anorexia Nervosa and Obesity: A Sense of Proportion* – in which he says:

> At one time drugs were extensively used, but it is now generally accepted that they have little part to play in treatment... Mega-tranquillisers like chlorpromazine are now given only to inpatients in hospitals where skilled nursing is in short supply and weight gain is slow ... Their great disadvantage is that they make the

patient drowsy, which she sometimes bitterly resents, and they are liable to have serious side-effects... There are no drugs that can make a persistent anorexic eat without external pressure and encouragement.

He also advises:

Coercion should never be used... If the anorexic is to be helped she must co-operate in the treatment, and that requires trust in the therapist and a say in what happens to her; in other words, to accept some responsibility for herself. If all control is taken from her she will certainly put on weight, but the chances are that she will lose it again once she regains her freedom...

Dally goes on to warn: 'Not everyone has the temperament and understanding to cope with such patients. The inpatient's refusal to eat can arouse considerable anger and aggression in doctors and nurses.'

Not that I could pretend that I was a model patient. Nor that I was normal. On 28 January, after being in All Saints for a fortnight (having been weighed-in at six stone), I wrote in my diary: 'Reached visitors' target [ie the weight at which I was allowed to receive visitors]: 45 kilos.' We were always weighed in kilos, perhaps in the hope that we would not understand what it meant; 45 kilos equals seven stone two pounds. 'Not a bit pleased – has not solved anything and feel VERY HEAVY AND FAT. DON'T want to put any more weight on.' The next entry (3 February) reads: 'Terrible day... real muddle – awfully upset – seem to be getting nowhere.'

I wonder whether this refers to the occasion when a family session had been called, attended by me, my parents, the various social workers and psychiatrists on my case. I don't recall exactly what was said, but the meeting very soon degenerated into a row between my father and the hospital, with me sitting in the middle wondering what on earth was going on. Only now, so many years later, in talking about this book with my father have I discovered that he was so horrified by my treatment – he felt it was 'inhuman' – that he had been compelled to say so. He could speak with some experience: as a hospital chaplain he had very often dealt with mental health patients. He wanted to get me out of there, but he didn't know where else to find help for me; help which he knew from his work as a pastor I desperately needed. I, of course, never really understood this, thinking only that he was ashamed of me.

'Wore clothes for first time since came in – felt really odd.' On the following day, I wrote: 'Another horrible day – restless and confused and heavy. Putting on weight DOES NOT solve a thing.'

I have only just rediscovered this diary. There's a list of figures on the blank pages at the back that I at first thought was some kind of cash register. On reading it more closely, however, I realised it was a record of my weight taken every day from 14 January (40.75 kilos) to 11 March (50.4 kilos). Any loss meant a withdrawal of privileges. You might well ask, how could we have lost anything while eating all that food? But we did. And as soon as we were sent home for the weekend, the losses were huge. I lost two and a half kilos (almost half a stone) in two days: 'HOME on weekend leave – terrified at the prospect.'

After some weeks I was allowed out with some of the other patients to go to a jumble sale in Chelsea. We were a very mixed bunch – anorexics, aged from 12 to 30, middle-aged ladies coming off alcohol, and a teenage boy who seemed perfectly normal to me except that he was very upset when Elvis died. (Disconcertingly, I realise now that since Elvis died in August 1977 I could not possibly have witnessed and been puzzled by the depth of his grief, as by then I had long since left All Saints.) I don't remember anything about the sale, but I can still see the long brick wall we walked beside on the way to the Underground and hear the thunderous noise of the traffic as it rushed past me. I felt as if the wall was about to crush me. It frightened me. Rather than learning how to eat, I had become so much worse that I was scared even to walk along the street. I discharged myself, weighing just under eight stone: I had put on two stone – 28 pounds – in less than eight weeks.

Did the wall really exist? Or had I also distorted this in my memory? I went to find it. It is still there, running alongside the gardens of the Imperial War Museum. As I walked beside it, dried-up sycamore leaves, blown by the wind, rattled their death-knell along the pavement behind me. I felt as if I was being prodded sharply in the back. My legs and arms seemed suddenly to have shrunk back to what they once were, and I knew that I was walking in the stiff, jerky, tense way that was me, Kate Chisholm, anorexic.

***

Anorexia begins with the inability of an individual to accept the changes necessary to becoming adult. It usually sets in as girls (or boys) are faced with the inevitable onset of maturation, although women who have married and had children do become anorexic, as do the elderly. But essentially it remains the same: a revolt against the adult world. As such, it is a provocation; not just to the family with whom the anorexic is at odds, but to society itself, daring as anorexics do to spurn its well-fed complacency.

To attempt to survive without food is an affront; an affront that is constantly in view. The skeletal body of an anorexic is both pathetic and defiant, arousing sympathy and hostility. In the cathedral at Norwich (home, coincidentally, to the Eating Disorders Association) there is a gruesome engraving of a skeleton on one of the side walls. It covers the grave of Thomas Gooding, who died in 1600. Beneath the crude outline are the words:

> All you that do this place pass bye
> Remember death for you must dye
> As you are now even so was I
> And as I am so shall you be
> Thomas Gooding here do staye
> Waiting for God's judgement daye

To come across this while wandering along the tranquil aisles of an Anglican cathedral is like being hit in the stomach. It's a brutal reminder of one's mortality. You, too, must die. And something about the way an anorexic reduces herself to skin and bone is a hostile reminder that you, too, are nothing but skin and bone. You, too, must die.

When I phoned an NHS eating-disorders clinic to inquire what kind of treatment programmes were available and spoke to the unit manager, she was at first very willing to help – until I explained that I had once been anorexic and was now writing a book which would try to describe the thoughts and feelings of an anorexic, 'Because it's very difficult for carers and professionals to understand what it feels like.'

She was outraged. 'It would be very dangerous to write a book like that.'

'But why?' I asked.

'It's very irresponsible. It might deter anorexics from coming forward for treatment. It's really not a good idea. Anorexia is a very serious psychiatric disorder. We're compassionate. We have a very good understanding of it. I really don't want to see a book that says we don't understand.'

What she said was valid – but why did my innocent statement provoke such a reaction? Why *should* other people 'understand' something so self-destructive and antisocial? Her antagonism reminded me of the aggression that I had encountered while I was ill. Perhaps, then, I had not imagined it? Maybe the odd reactions my not-eating aroused were something for which *I* was not responsible? Maybe they were not part of *my* illness?

In not-eating, the anorexic is not simply refusing to grow up. She is in part driven by her inability to accept that the world is full of imperfections. As she lies in her hospital bed, near to death, reduced to a mere skeletal form of her own deliberate making, she is reminding all those around her of their own mortality. But not only this; she is also in some underhand way forcing them to acknowledge the compromises they have made as adults. By not-eating, the anorexic is refusing to go along with the pretence that life is essentially benevolent, or to accept the terms of whatever adult life is available to her. And to do so is to discomfit and disturb, reminding others that perhaps their lives are not as fulfilled or as contented as they would like to believe, or pretend, them to be.

It is frightening for parents to watch helplessly as their daughter changes from the seemingly happy, equable, achieving girl they once knew to the with-drawn, miserable and often aggrieved little person with whom they can make no contact. It's frighten-ing – and also alienating. Not surprisingly, most par-ents find it almost impossible to deal with. And so do many professionals.

***

I walked back to Lambeth North station and took the Underground to Barons Court so that I could revisit the Charing Cross Hospital, where, five months after leaving All Saints, I had landed up, weighing less than five stone. This time, a friend of my parents who happened to play golf with a con-sultant who treated anorexics arranged for me to go and see him. Dr Winsom took one look at me and said, 'You had better come into my ward.'

The sun had completely disappeared and thick grey clouds loured above the tower block that is the hospital. When I first arrived there in August 1977, it was still quite new and an extraordinary contrast to All Saints. More like a hotel than a hospital, with shops on the ground floor, swanky lifts, and arty paintings on the walls.

I took the lift to the ninth floor (the call-buttons had been changed; for some reason I remember them exactly, maybe because the lifts were my escape route). Ward Nine North is now an elderly patients' psychiatric ward. 'Welcome to the West London Mental Health Trust' announces a banner above the door. I pushed the buzzer and a dumpy Slavic woman with rosy cheeks and black hair streaked with grey, drawn tightly back into a ponytail, looked grumpily at me through the window in the door before letting me in.

Is she a nurse? I wondered. She was not in uniform and did not speak English very fluently. I explained that I had made an arrangement by phone to visit the ward. She did not seem to comprehend what I was saying, and so I began to tell her that I had been here, on the ward, in that room over there, 20-odd years ago. She looked even more confused, and obviously hadn't understood a word.

Another 'nurse' (also not in uniform) told me to sit down and to wait for Rosa with whom I had made the arrangement. She, too, did not seem to take in what I was saying.

'I used to be on this ward. In that room. I was here for seven months.'

A blank expression again. Beginning to realise

how odd my visit must have seemed to her, I tried to explain: 'This used to be a ward for anorexics. I was here then. About 20 years ago.'

Blank expression.

'I was anorexic.'

'Ah, anorexic. I used to nurse them. About three years ago. The Gordon Hospital. All very beautiful girls. I don't know. Why wouldn't they eat?' She leaned towards me, conspiratorially, 'What treatment?'

My turn to go blank. What *had* been the regime under Dr Winsom? I couldn't think where to begin. Stuffed with food? Weighed endlessly? No baths? That's all I could remember – that, and of course the days and months of doing nothing, absolutely nothing, except to worry obsessively about what I would next have to eat.

To be fair, my treatment at the Charing Cross was very different from All Saints. Bed rest and a system of treats and punishments prevailed, but the regime was much gentler. Dr Winsom was an endocrinologist, not a psychiatrist. He had developed a team that had been very successful at treating anorexics from a medical, rather than psychiatric, point of view. But this was at the old Charing Cross Hospital, and he had not been able to recreate its special environment in the new, high-tech ward, where most of his patients were diabetic not anorexic.

He tried everything with me, bar drugs. I was allowed to choose what I ate (well, at least, between the three options on the daily NHS menu), given sherry before meals to help my appetite (it was kept on the drugs trolley), and sent to the gym for physiotherapy to rebuild my wasted muscles. As soon as I was strong enough, I was allowed out on afternoon walks with other patients (I made friends with the diabetics, avoiding the few anorexics who came and went during my seven-month stay).

An old schoolfriend came to visit and agreed to have me to stay for the weekend to see whether I was ready to eat in company. I wasn't. Eating, to me, was associated with her happy life. I was different. Something had slipped out of focus; and, it seemed, would never slip back again.

As we sat in her kitchen, talking about our English A-level teacher, I looked at the food on the plate, and it was as if I had to climb an insurmountable mountain just to eat a small portion of it. Better not even to begin, and to refuse everything. I never thought about how she must have felt; never considered how my refusal to accept help must have been upsetting to everyone around me.

At Charing Cross, they did not try to push psychotherapy, analysis, counselling, family therapy on me, knowing how I had resisted everything that had been offered by All Saints. But they did once send me to the hospital psychiatrist – an odd-looking woman with wig-like hair, who sat behind a desk in what I remember as being a very long room. She advised me to go and look at the male nudes in the British Museum. I thought at the time that she was barmy. How could looking at statues of nude men help me to cope with life? But when I first saw Sam Taylor-Wood's video of the dancing male at the opening of Tate Modern, some 23 years later, I began to see what she might have meant. Why be so wary of one's physical being?

In a way, I was lucky to have been treated by Dr Winsom and at Charing Cross, where I was indulged with enormous patience. On one occasion I was discovered *in flagrante*, tossing my extra portion of ice cream and jelly down the toilet in my room. The door had been locked but I found a way of twisting the lock open with a pair of needlework scissors. I spent the next three days, confined to bed, weeping quietly into my pillow.

Eventually, I was let off the hateful slab of red jelly and creamy-yellow ice cream melting through its wax-paper wrapper, but I put on very little weight. When I discharged myself in February 1978, I weighed almost the same as I had done when I first went into All Saints just over a year earlier. Nevertheless, I had got used to eating three times a day, and had been sufficiently out of the world to feel strong enough to face it all again.

I'm still reliving that experience when Rosa reappears to chivvy me on. It is time to leave, but I still haven't been inside my old room. Maybe I should take a look, whether they like it or not. I get up. 'Can I just take a quick look?'

'Of course.'

I stand by the window looking out on to what used to be the Harrods depository on the other side of the river – a huge, red-brick, turreted warehouse. It was odd to see that view again.

Enough memories. I turn away and walk out.

6. CIVIL WAR

The therapist has an uphill struggle trying to get them to talk of their feelings, moods and humours, and often gets nowhere at all.
Mara Selvini Palazzoli, *Self-Starvation*

The question is how to persuade, trick, bribe or force a negativistic patient into doing what she is determined not to do, and how to achieve this without doing more psychological damage.
Hilde Bruch, *The Golden Cage*

When in April 2000 the government called a Body Image Summit to discuss with eating disorders experts, writers on feminist issues, model agencies and women's magazine editors what should be done about the rising number of young girls (and boys) who are suffering from the ever-increasing variety of eating disorders, the outcome was a promise by the magazine editors and model agencies to stop promoting pictures of ultra-thin women.

Two years on, models still look like stick insects (even Sophie Dahl, once proud of her majestic proportions, has given in and gone on a diet), and the real story of eating disorders and how many people suffer from them has yet to be told. On the weekend before Christmas 2001, a *Sunday Times* magazine article headlined that there are 6,000 new cases of anorexia each year. But where did this figure come from? I rang the Eating Disorders Association and was told that detailed statistics just do not exist; it all depends on how you define 'eating disorder' and 'severely anorexic'.

What is known for sure is that in the UK there are only 39 NHS specialist units and 18 private clinics dedicated to eating disorders, with about 150 inpatient beds. And these are so unevenly distributed that 50 per cent of regional health authorities have no specialist units within their area. Most anorexics are cared for at home, looked after by their families or partners; and for them it's a nightmare. 'It's like living with a nutter,' one mother told me.

It's not so much our obsession with thinness that needs to be remedied – although if we went back to believing that curvaceous was good and bony was bad we might all be happier. Nor does there seem much point in dedicating endless articles – in the medical journals just as much as in women's maga-zines – to discussions of whether or not we are wit-nessing an epidemic of eating disorders. Far more necessary is a critical assessment of the treatment currently available, and whether it can be made more effective.

Anorexia is so difficult to treat because it is both a medical and psychiatric condition. How do you persuade a dangerously malnourished but fiercely resistant person to eat, without imposing some kind of reward-and-punishment regime? How do you deal with the fact that food is not the real issue when the presenting patient is in clinical danger from self-starvation? On the one hand, the anorexic is desperate for someone to take over and make all her decisions for her, especially about eating; on the other hand, she bitterly resents any attempt to control her. 'Anorexia,' said the eating disorders expert Professor Arthur Crisp, 'is neither primarily a psychotic illness nor an organic disease, but perhaps its echoes of both are responsible for some of the enigma it presents.'

When the Royal College of Psychiatrists commissioned a survey in August 2001 – 'Eating Disorders in the UK: Policies for Service Development and Training' – the published report observed that many of the staff in specialist units had received no special training in the treatment of patients with this 'unique mixture of psychiatric, physical and psychosocial problems'. Is it any wonder then that patients prove resistant to treatment?

I was first diagnosed in 1977, when anorexia nervosa was rarely heard of or written about. There were specialist units attached to some of the teaching hospitals, but anorexic patients, if their illness was properly diagnosed, usually found themselves either in a high-security mental hospital, sometimes having been sectioned under the Mental Health Act, or on a general medical ward where no one quite knew why they were taking up bed-space. I was treated first by a psychiatrist and then by a physician. Each tried their best, but neither was able to provide a course of treatment that dealt with all aspects of the illness, with my need both to eat *and* to learn how to combat my inability to cope with life.

Nowadays the treatment options, if they are available, vary widely from inpatient refeeding programmes to outpatient counselling, via cognitive behaviour and family therapies. At Rhodes Farm, for instance – a private, 32-bed clinic in north London founded by Dr Dee Dawson for anorexic children aged between six and 16 – the approach is simple. 'This is a boarding-school rather than a hospital,' declares its website. The children are kept as busy as possible during the day, so that they have little time to become preoccupied with what they are eating. There is no bed-rest regime, no withdrawal of privileges, and at the beginning therapeutic intervention is limited to one session a week.

Every child/patient must gain one kilo every week; if they fail in one week, they have to put on two kilos in the next, so that it is possible 'to predict accurately the discharge date'. Rhodes Farm, says the website, will not charge health authorities 'for any weeks where the patients do not gain one kilo'.

Rapid restoration of eating is of vital importance to young teenagers whose growth will be impeded by prolonged starvation. And using peer-group pressure – the patients eat together at Rhodes Farm and no one is allowed to leave the table until everyone has finished – works for some people. But what if it doesn't? Not much room for individuality here, or for an understanding of what is going on in the anorexic's mind. Having said that, with young teenagers, where the negative habits of thought are not yet so entrenched, such a short, sharp rehabilitation will often have a lasting effect.

With other patients, recovery may depend on sorting out the family dynamic that has gone wrong. Mara Selvini Palazzoli developed strategies for treatment after close observation of her anorexic patients in session with their families. In *Self-Starvation*, she describes how she and her colleagues would then devise a behavioural solution – what she refers to as 'a ritual' – involving every member of the family.

One family, for example, was told to shut the front door to all visitors after dinner and to stay seated round the table for an hour. Every family member was then to speak for 15 minutes (strictly timed) in order of seniority. No one was to interrupt or contradict and whatever was said was not to be repeated outside the ritual hour. The family had to do this on alternate nights for a fortnight. It worked. The anorexic, who was gravely ill and had attempted suicide, learnt that many of her resentments about her extended family, who visited incessantly and had too much influence on her parents, were justified and were not because she was spiteful and not a good daughter. Once her parents and sister had begun to express themselves honestly and to respect each other's point of view, so her eating problems receded until they became unimportant to her.

Family therapy is available in the UK – at the Maudsley in south London, for instance, Christopher Dare and Ivan Eisler, working with a team of clinicians and researchers, have devised a method of treatment which gives to the family the responsibility for nurturing their seriously ill child back to health. The method involves three phases of treatment, from initial refeeding, which is accomplished by the family strongly backed by the team of therapists, through encouraging the parents to give more control to the anorexic over what she should eat, and finally enabling the patient to maintain a stable weight without any parental supervision. The initial work with the family is very time-consuming; what works with one, will not necessarily work for another. But, once the inner workings of the family are uncovered, recovery can be accomplished remarkably quickly.

I'm not sure how I would have reacted to such an approach – probably with great hostility, as I did not believe that my family was in any way involved with my illness. But the willingness to react to the individual circumstances of the patient rather than to impose on her a treatment strategy can only be beneficial.

In recent years the emphasis in the NHS has been on the provision of day-care centres and outpatient clinics. Clare Lindsay describes in her book, *Conquering Anorexia,* the treatment she received at a day hospital in North Yorkshire, and why it worked for her. She had been anorexic for over seven years since she was 13, but recovered – in five months – to the point where she is now able to manage her weight without relapse. For her, working with the other patients (mostly not anorexics) in rigidly ordered days of counselling, group therapy, drama, art, stress management and swimming helped her to restructure and redirect her life, and she was able to find a new purpose and confidence in herself as a person.

But not everyone will respond to day-care. It's not enough for them – especially since most of the therapy available is not specific to eating disorders. At the Hope Seminar, I met Ruth, who was an outpatient at a specialist unit in London. She was tiny – very short, painfully thin, childlike in her manner. I was shocked to learn that she was actually 23 and not the 13-year-old I thought her to be. Not trusted to travel to the Bethlem by herself, both her parents had brought her. She was having counselling and taking part in art and drama therapy. But she had only gained a couple of pounds in six months and could see no reason to put on any more.

It was pitiful to hear her little, apologetic voice, and to watch the shy, retiring, I-am-not-here expressions flit across her pinched face. Life was comfortable in her fortress; no need to face up to adult life. In a way she looked quite well – until you realised she was meant by now to be a young woman. Then her childishness seemed grotesquely sad. Another wasted life.

As Hilde Bruch has warned: 'Often the symptoms [of not-eating] lose their dynamic significance and become nearly automatic, and patients will incorporate them in their sense of identity... when the condition reaches this stage it may be inaccessible to psychotherapeutic intervention.' That is why inpatient treatment is sometimes necessary, both to take the anorexic out of the setting in which she has become ill, and to provide the kind of intensive care that is needed to support her in her fight against the illness (for that is how treatment should be conducted: as a joint effort against a common enemy).

Most of the inpatient units in the UK are attached to mental hospitals, some still in their original Victorian buildings. The eating disorders unit at the Bethlem in south London is set within the huge estate of wooded parkland that belongs to the hospital. It's peaceful, plenty of space for walking, but it is isolated and institutional, with locked doors and high-wire fencing. To me, it felt forbidding, alienating and reinforcing of the mind-set: I am different, I am set apart from the world, I am at war with those who are trying to persuade me to eat.

That said, the treatment regime is very different from those used in the past. 'Motivational enhancement therapy', which aims to neutralise the patient's negative response by involving her in making choices about how she is treated, has replaced reward-and-punishment. If a patient says she does not like being weighed twice a week (close monitoring is essential for very low-weight patients), she is weighed with her back to the scales so that she cannot see what is being recorded. Every attempt is made to put the anorexic back in control of what happens to her; she attends her own case conferences and is encouraged to comment on how she feels about her progress.

Hope Seminars are organised regularly to bring inpatients and outpatients together with the staff caring for them to discuss the illness and how best to treat it. This is a tremendous breakthrough for any anorexic – to be able to talk about being ill. I could never have done it, because I didn't really believe that I was ill, and in any case I had no idea how to express what I felt. At the seminar I attended, I was amazed to hear anorexics of all ages speaking out about what was wrong with them.

But at the same time I could not help noticing the difference in outlook between the inpatients and those who were just there for the day. We had all come to find out more about what could be done to help those with eating problems, and the atmosphere was one of co-operation rather than of medical staff on one side and patients on the other. And yet, while the outpatients were willing to accept that help was available and could make a difference, the inpatients were fierce and antagonistic in their every gesture. They sat apart and, when they did speak, it was only to interrupt with negative comments. This was, of course, partly because they were at a different stage of the illness. But how much was their attitude a reaction to being confined in an institution?

When I first walked into All Saints, I was desperate for someone to help me to eat. I had no idea what was going on inside my head, no suspicion that as soon as I put on even a pound of weight an all-out war would begin between me and the medical staff. Until that first meal – and the reaction of the nurse – I had been disturbed, puzzled and confused by my reluctance to eat and my pleasure in losing weight, but I had not (as far as I recall) been actively aggressive in my determination to not-eat. As soon as I was made to see that eating was my problem, I resisted all forms of treatment. It was, I believed, the only way I could preserve my integrity. And everything that happened subsequently confirmed me in that view: my very being was under siege.

Penny Baily, the parent of a child who was once severely ill with anorexia, set up her own clinic because of her determination to find a successful way of treating the illness. She believes that the optimum environment for recovery is a medical unit, with a high level of individual support, but within a comfortable, as-near-as-normal homely atmosphere where patients can feel safe. And so she bought a large Edwardian house on the outskirts of Norwich and converted it into Newmarket House. 'Gentle re-feeding' is combined with therapy that is designed to help the patients begin to take responsibility for their own eating. All staff receive specialist training in dealing with anorexics. Patients are either referred via the NHS or contact the clinic direct.

This appears to be a fantastically expensive treatment option: it costs £270 a day for the NHS to keep a patient at Newmarket House, and the average length of stay is seven months. But although it does take months of patient (and expensive) rebuilding to undo the years of damage inflicted by anorexia, those months may well prevent a lifetime of relapses, and, in terms of the NHS budget, be more cost-effective.

The one-on-one care and daily timetable of activities at Newmarket House could be seen as authoritarian (and no doubt is regarded as such by many patients) – never having a moment to yourself – but it is reassuring too. The patients are never left alone to dwell endlessly on the misery of being made to eat, and thereby giving in to the 'authority' figures. And this is why inpatient care is so essential for those who have become severely anorexic. Once you have been forced by your increasing weakness to embark on some kind of treatment programme, then the war against anorexia really begins. The voices inside your head just never stop, invading every waking moment and even your dreams, one minute telling you to eat, to go for life, and the next warning you that to eat and put on weight will mean facing up to the things you are so desperately trying to avoid.

I arranged to visit Newmarket House, intrigued and yet also fearful. Would it bring back memories of what I had experienced in hospital? Quite the reverse. I was astonished to meet girls with smiles on their faces and colour in their cheeks. Despite their skeletal thinness, cleverly disguised by oversized jumpers and baggy jeans, there was an air of normality about the place; indeed it was often difficult to tell who was the carer and who the patient. Anorexia is a claustrophobic illness, the personality smothered and cramped by all those bad feelings, and this is heightened and reinforced by being enclosed in an institution. At Newmarket House, with its colourful decor and large, airy rooms with huge windows, there is space to breathe and open up like a bud in spring after a winter of being frosted into dormancy.

Only very severely ill anorexics are referred to Newmarket House by the NHS; some, in their forties, have been in and out of eating disorders clinics since their teens. Such patients are lucky: compared with what's on offer in an NHS hospital, Newmarket House is like a luxury hotel (lunch was being cooked while I was there, and I couldn't help but notice that it smelt delicious: all home-made, with vegetables fresh from the garden).

But money is not the only reason for its hopeful outlook. A different kind of therapeutic engagement has been adopted here (as it has at the Bethlem), in which patients are shown from the outset that food is not the central issue. For anorexia is not about food, calories, pounds and ounces; not really. And the question for those caring for an anorexic is not How Can We Make Her Eat? But How Can We Make Her Feel That She Is Worth The Bother Of Trying To Eat?

Once you are inside that fortress, it is so much easier to remain there than to fight your way out. The illness is also very dangerous, and becoming more so with the advent of the computer highway. It is now possible to chat to other anorexics on the internet whose impersonality is the perfect retreat for an anti-social not-eater. Pro-anorexia societies have been formed, whose web-talking members, the 'Annas' – Anorexics for Anorexia – are campaigning for the legal right to choose not to eat, to resist all forms of treatment, and to offer advice on how to reduce your weight to five stone and beyond in as many weeks.

Such chatlines and advice columns would never work outside the web; face-to-face there could never be such unity. Everyone would be vying for the right to say 'I am the thinnest of you all.'

'At least we are not risking any lives here,' one of the Annas is reported to have said in their defence. 'If we want to die this way, then that should be our choice.' The language is reminiscent of those medieval fasting saints, except that the word 'God' has been replaced by 'I'. This is no holy fast, but an obstinate refusal to make terms with life. And this is why the Annas must be resisted. The trouble with choosing anorexia as the locus of your ambition is obvious: you can never succeed unless through death. Absolute success requires absolute negation.

Although anorexics always present with the same symptoms, the reasons for their illness are complex and very individual. The way out is also very individual. As the Royal College of Psychiatrists recommended, more specialist services are needed, and these services must provide a combination of outpatient, inpatient and day-patient care. An 'appropriate range of therapeutic interventions' must be made available, suiting the treatment to the individual rather than vice versa.

Anorexics are horribly resistant to everything that is offered them. But it is important to remember always that behind that aggressive attitude is a terrified little girl – or boy (for every ten female anorexics, there is one male). What an anorexic wants most is reassurance, but she will never allow herself to say (or be able to admit to herself) that she needs help. It's like approaching a dangerous animal: stealth and intelligent tactics are required.

7. RESOLUTION

OK, you need willpower to become anorexic, but you need about 100 times more to come out of it again. Only you can do it, you see. They can't do it for you.

Lucy, quoted by Morag MacSween in *Anorexic Bodies*

Nobody, who has not been in the interior of a family, can say what the difficulties of any individual of that family may be.

Jane Austen, *Emma*

'Become aware of your body; your whole body; your *whole* body. Become aware of your body and your contact with the ground. Be very aware of your body, of every part of your body, and of your contact with the ground…'

It is April 1996, and I am lying flat on the floor in the back row of a roomful of yoga students and I am feeling very self-conscious. It's my first time, and I'm not comfortable with the idea of being asked to pay close attention to my body, and to listen to what it, rather than my mind, is telling me. Me, a one-time anorexic, who has spent most of her adult years disliking her body.

Not that I am any longer anorexic. I have been off it for years. My weight is normal, and my only quirk regarding food is my refusal to eat meat. But I am still haunted by the ghosts of anorexia and by my shame that I once allowed it to take over. I have learnt to live with my body as it is, but never to like it, or to wish to spend any time thinking about it. I never weigh myself; there's only one small mirror in my flat, and that's not in the bathroom. I still don't like my curves, but I put up with them, knowing that it is better to accept them than to revert back into not-eating to remove them.

'Become aware of your body…' Is it really possible to be aware of your body and be relaxed? I don't think so. My way of getting over anorexia has been to try to forget about how I feel and to busy myself with living. But as I slowly begin to learn the techniques of stretching, breathing and focusing on the experience of the present moment, I discover that it is possible to be self-conscious of your body and not be disturbed by this; to reach a point where the body and the mind are still and in a state of peace – even if only for a moment.

Yoga brings the body, mind and spirit into balance, striking at the very heart of the anorexic mindset and its adamant refusal to listen to the body's demands. I'm not sure if yoga would have helped me when my anorexia was at its worst, but I like to think that it might have done. Simply stretching your arms and legs, with awareness and in accordance with your breathing, brings real calm to both body and mind; something that it is impossible for the restless, starved, weak anorexic to achieve otherwise. In such a tranquil state – even if it only lasts for a second or two – a moment of insight, the possibility of change, might occur. And yet only rarely is yoga included in treatment programmes for anorexics. Why not also teach it in schools? Yoga would introduce vulnerable teenagers to practical ways of combating those acute feelings of self-loathing and bad body image.

Of course, there is much other work to be done; the negative thought patterns of the anorexic cannot be neutralised overnight. And this must be understood from the outset: there is no quick-fix cure. It will take years of dogged persistence before an anorexic is reconciled to herself and to eating just like everyone else. As Lucy, an anorexic quoted by Morag MacSween in *Anorexic Bodies*, explains, 'OK, you need willpower to become anorexic, but you need about 100 times more to come out of it again.' That I am sure is why so many give up: it is easier to continue not-eating than to eat. Once you have trained yourself so rigorously to refuse food, it takes an awful lot of energy to retrain yourself to eat anything and everything. And the anorexic demons know just when to re-attack, tempting you back into your old ways.

Although I did painstakingly rebuild a life for myself, I was never completely free of the negative thoughts that had led me into anorexia in the first place. I could never forget what I had done, or escape the feeling that I am not like other people; that I must be peculiarly temperamental and diffi-cult, otherwise I would never have put myself and all those around me through such trauma. And yet a bit of me also knew that I had learnt from all those years of not-quite-living. There is some compensa-tion for all that wasted time – self-knowledge.

At the end of her book, *Conversations with Anorexics*, Hilde Bruch says of one of her patients that, 'In spite of the pain and suffering that the anorexia had caused, she felt that it had played a positive role in her life; that without it she might have been stuck with her overdependent attitude towards her family.'

It may seem like an odd thing to say. How can all that suffering be worth it? But it can, it really can –

as long as the experience is used, rather than abused.

Karen Margolis, whose book *To Eat or Not to Eat* charts her own battle with anorexia when she was in her late twenties, writes, 'Do not pity me. Part of me enjoyed it.' She admits that she used the illness as a weapon. 'It was, after all, highly effective: it forced many people to pay attention to my needs.' But at the same time 'it forced my family, especially my parents, to a crisis of confrontation that we may not have reached another way, and that I needed.' It's a drastic way to find out who you really are, but sometimes it is the only way.

The trouble is that the anorexic will need to summon up all her reserves of courage, while those around her will need to be equally resilient and superhumanly patient, if resolution is to be attained. And, as Gill Todd, clinical nurse leader at the Bethlem, explained to us at the Hope Seminar, relapse is an integral part of the process. We discussed the way that the illness progresses through a cycle that was common to us all (following the description given by Charles Lasègue all those years ago) – from being pernickety about food to outright resistance and collapse, followed by temporary recovery. The anorexic may have to go through this cycle as many as eight times before she is strong enough physically and mentally to opt permanently for Exit; learning how to live without the comfort of not-eating.

**

I have been out of hospital for almost two years and am back in Edinburgh, striving to make a new life for myself. At home in London I had been managing to keep my weight at about seven stone (by eating the same thing every day: scrambled egg, toast and carrot salad) and had held down a job for a year. But then I took the plunge of leaving and attempting to survive on my own without family or close friends.

It's too soon; although reconciled to eating, I am not prepared to take responsibility for myself, and have no idea how to make myself eat a meal every day. A cousin offers me the use of her flat, and occasionally she is there as well, but I am usually on my own. I don't have a job, but assume I will be able to get enough work as a temp even though I know no shorthand. On one surreal job I find myself manning a four-board, plug-operated switchboard in a huge computer factory without a clue how to do it.

I survive just two days. The rest of the time I help out at the National Union of Students' office. It's strange to be back among students after what I have been through; I feel so old, and out of touch.

I'm soon plummeting right back into losing weight and taking pride in it. On several occasions I remember eating a whole boiled beetroot for supper: it's piping hot, staves off the hunger pangs without adding calories, and I just can't face up to the necessity of cooking and eating a proper meal by myself. But this time I begin to feel pretty ill very quickly. My body is tired of running on empty, and that bitter east-coast wind cuts straight through me.

Travelling home for Christmas, I end up on a British Rail train that leaves Waverley station on a freezing December dawn with no heating and no chance of a hot drink: the buffet staff haven't turned up. By the time we reach the outskirts of Birmingham, where we sit and wait for a signal, it is an hour and a half late and I realise that I will miss my connection to Reading, where my father has arranged for me to be met by someone I do not know. I am frozen both inside and out, weak because I have eaten nothing since the night before, and have no idea how to get a message through that

I am going to be late. (This is the low-tech 1970s, so no mobile phones.) Tears well up and I can feel them slowly trickling down my sallow cheeks.

At that moment, I see myself as I must look to the other passengers: a grown woman crying because she has missed a train; a painfully thin, childlike woman with a miserable, unappealing face; a paper graduate with years of education behind her who can't find her way home.

In that same instant, I see also an earlier version of myself on another journey, arriving at Istanbul airport with a rucksack, my head full of visions of the golden capital of Byzantium. No one there to meet me, and all roads into the city blocked by a cavalcade of armoured trucks on their way to fight the Greeks in Cyprus. Where is that excited, resourceful girl now?

I feel ashamed that I have allowed myself to become so pathetic. But not just ashamed. For the first time, I am angry with myself, too. At last, a positive, energising emotion (my godmother used to tell me I should think of it as 'divine discontent'). It is as if a reality button deep within me has somehow been switched on again, and I can see that unless I do something – and very soon – I'm going to be back inside hospital, and so it will go on, and on, and on.

A life spent in and out of hospital, being forced unwillingly to eat.

I see clearly what I have become, and that the only person who can help me is myself. Unless, and until, I choose to get well, no one can help me out of this misery. No one else can lead me back to the person I once was, and want to be again; only I know that she existed. And, for a while, I believe that I can do it.

I stumble off the train, and somehow meet up with my family (I don't remember how), and begin to eat (I do recall that first meal – sausages and baked beans). Turkey, bacon, mince-pies, roast parsnips – and cheese sandwiches between every meal. The enthusiasm is short-lived. Having made the decision to eat anything and everything, just like everyone else, so my anorexic self struggles to reassert itself. It is the most difficult time for my family. I argue continually with myself and with them throughout every minute of the day, trying to decide what and how much I should eat. Am I being greedy? Will I go on and on putting on weight? Will my body know when to stop demanding all this extra food? But I'm spurred on always by the memory of that unlikely moment on a BR train stalled in the outskirts of Birmingham. In nine months, I *put on two stone – this time by my own choice.*

***

The flash of understanding is an experience common to many sufferers; when, for no apparent reason, the kaleidoscope suddenly shifts, letting in the light after weeks, months, years of being stuck in-between views. Actually what happens is a very gradual accretion of self-knowledge, which creeps up on you unawares. All those interminable conversations with doctors, nurses, family, friends – which they probably thought had gone unheard and unacknowledged – do have an effect; the drip-drip-drip of water on impacted rock.

I found myself a job back in London, and a room in a flatshare in Earl's Court with an old university friend. I was back on course. The blips that followed were minor; but blips there always were, although something always prevented me from allowing myself to get so low that I had to go back into hospital. Alarm-bells would start ringing in my head as soon as I became aware that I was taking pride in my increasingly concave stomach. It was as if some unconscious mechanism was triggered every time I declined to a certain weight or paralysed state of mind, and I just knew that I had to make myself eat something. In fact, I became just as scared of losing weight as I had once been of putting it on.

I learned to accept that although I was no longer outwardly anorexic, somewhere deep inside it still lurked, waiting to grab hold of me again. I never forgot my experience on that train to Reading via Birmingham, but it was also true that I never confronted the 'inner psychological orientation', as Hilde Bruch once described it, that had led me into anorexia. I needed to learn how to look at the bad feelings without flinching; only then would they lose their potency.

Felicia, who was treated by Bruch after becoming anorexic while she was a student, wrote to her psychotherapist many years later:

> I don't want to let you believe that everything is just 'perfect' now – I do occasionally find myself having to stop and look at some of the old relics that I carry around in a deep 'hidden back pocket' of me still. But each time this happens, I seem to be able to rather quickly 'dust off' the relic, clean it of the rationalisation of fear, or anger, or doubts that make it seem 'a valuable possession' and then retire it to its pocket again.

I'm not sure that you can ever get rid totally of the 'old relics' of behaviour and feeling that once made you anorexic. Like an old scar after an operation or accident, which becomes red and itchy in bad weather but never reopens, the relics will impinge on your consciousness from time to time. They are part of who you are. But you can ensure that they no longer have any power over you – just as in meditation you don't engage with the unbidden thoughts that threaten to distract you, but rather allow them to pass through your mind without engaging with them.

The problem with so much of the treatment received by those anorexics fortunate enough to be diagnosed and offered something more than simply weight-gain regimes is the way that the therapies attempt to reprogramme the individual according to a pre-set module. This is rather like giving a face-lift to a patient who is dissatisfied with the way she is ageing. The wrinkles may be ironed out superficially, but they will continue to crease and rumple underneath.

Susie Orbach's latest book, *On Eating* (marketed as a self-help manual), offers tips on how to be at ease with your eating urges. She outlines five keys to good eating – Eat When You Are Hungry, Eat the

Food Your Body Is Hungry For, Find Out Why You Eat When You Aren't Hungry, Taste Every Mouthful, Stop Eating the Moment You Are Full. She poses the question: My family wants me to eat with them and to eat what they are eating, but it doesn't suit me. What then should I do? Her response is that you should agree to sit with them while they eat but refuse to eat yourself, or, make everyone else eat what you want to eat 'so that they eat what you desire'. This could mean, according to Orbach's tips, eating pudding before the main course, since this will stop you gorging on sweet things, or leaving the meal in the middle of a course because you have had enough, or asking the restaurant to make you up a packet of sandwiches which you can eat later when you have built up an appetite.

Such tricks may well work if you live alone, never eat with friends, don't have a job, and have unlimited amounts to spend on food. But what if you don't? What is more: will they encourage you to make peace with your errant feelings? Pride is the besetting sin of the anorexic: pride in her self-denial, in her thin body, in her superiority to those around her, in her ability to survive alone (well, at least until she collapses). It is the task of the therapist to break through, and break down, this carapace *without* destroying the kernel of selfhood inside.

I always resisted fiercely any hint of reprogramming, fearing that in the process I would lose what was 'original' about me. I didn't trust the treatment I was being offered. This, of course, is part of the illness: once you are in that fortress, anyone who dares to approach is considered to be an enemy. But it was also because I was so often told 'This is what you are feeling', rather than being allowed to say for myself what was going on inside my head. I didn't want to be told that anger was at the root of what I felt; that this was obvious in my body language as I sat on the edge of the bed rigidly holding myself, elbows hugging my chest, ankles crossed. Or that I was dominated by my father, or my mother. In fact what I felt was a searing pain, as if I was undergoing surgery without anaesthetic. I held myself tightly to ease the pain, and because I was terrified that otherwise I would fall apart.

It would be so much easier, says Hilde Bruch, to explain away anorexia if the patient was from a family in which the father was an absentee drunkard and the mother scatty and herself in need of care. But although abuse, divorce or break-up have been experienced by some 30 per cent of anorexics (which is the same as in other psychiatric illnesses), most sufferers come from seemingly happy, achieving families. 'It is very hard,' explains Bruch, 'particularly for well-meaning parents, to understand the unhappiness from the subtle misunderstandings.' It's not that the family is dysfunctional, but that within it the anorexic feels oppressed and somehow not able to speak, or rather not able to let her real self speak out. Hypersensitive, she will have a fragile sense of who she is, and will overreact to any sort of criticism.

'These youngsters,' says Bruch, '...experience teasing as insults.' But, surely, teasing is normal in family life? Of course it is. But, for the anorexic, with her super-thin skin, any derogatory comment, however much said in fun, is dwelt on endlessly and obsessively. I would storm off in tears whenever anyone said anything about me that I didn't like or disagreed with. If a cake I had just baked was not as perfect as I had wished, I would react as if it were a major disaster – a reflection on my imperfection. This in itself is not unusual among difficult teenagers. But when combined with an inability to talk to anyone about what you are feeling, and a need to control everything around and within you, it is potent.

Hilde Bruch tells one of her patients, 'The great

painful experience, the great unhappiness and suffering of your childhood, was that you had nobody to complain to; and that there was nobody who acknowledged your complaints, your pain, as justified when you experienced them.' On the surface, the family may be functioning perfectly, with love and care for everyone, but, in their midst, the anorexic – who very often will have been the good child, the caring daughter, the child who never makes a fuss – will be unable to express what she is feeling. Without such expression, she cannot discover who she is.

This is not to say that no one listened to her, but that she perceived herself not to be heard, or not to be able to speak. Another family member may think back on things very differently; that in her experience the anorexic herself was always in control of what went on within the family. My sister, who is nine years younger than me, remembers mealtimes as being 'often dramatic and occasionally violent'. On one occasion, she says, a plate was thrown against the wall (I have no recollection of this). 'For a young teenager,' she says, 'it was difficult to understand all this fuss about food. Why did Mum go out every night to visit Kate, or Catherine as we used to call her, in hospital?

'I remember my brother's wedding with Kate just skin and bones, like a skeleton, in a red suit.' She felt that I got all of the attention and that she had to keep quiet. 'My little teenage issues were nothing in relation to the drama and emotion caused by Kate and food.'

As Mara Selvini Palazzoli says of her experience of dealing with anorexics, 'All these patients are stubbornly self-willed and rarely worry about the effects of their behaviour on the members of their family... They readily burst into tears at the least sign of opposition, often sobbing their hearts out in the privacy of their rooms, but occasionally causing dramatic scenes.'

Therapy has to help the patient find ways of expressing herself that are controlled and responsible. This involves a long and patient process. Every anorexic has come to the illness by a different route, for many, complex reasons. There is no simple exit from it, no single way out. And the patient has to find the way out herself. 'It is important that the patient... has a chance to say it first,' says Hilde Bruch. Only then will she be able to rebuild herself using her own strengths, not those imposed on her by the therapist.

What needs to be remembered is that anorexia is

not all bad. The willpower and determination, the sensitivity, the desire to be important to people, to always take on the caring role, the ability to withstand physical discomfort are all great virtues. But you need to learn how to use the good bits and discard the bad.

I never understood what had happened to me, and was always ashamed of what I had done to myself – and to my family. The whole subject was unmentionable, and best forgotten. This, I believe, is why, despite the huge number of books about eating disorders, there is so little literature that captures the inside world of an anorexic. It's just too painful and difficult to go back into that perverse mindset. And yet this is the kind of book that is most needed by those trying to cope with the extreme behaviour of a not-eater, to give them hope and understanding.

It is only as I have come now, very belatedly, to look at my anorexic tendencies with the detachment of an observer that I have seen that deep down, very deep down, I had never accepted that I needed to make the separation from family that I should have accomplished in my teens. As Monty Don, who suffered from anorexia in his late teens and early twenties, has written: 'No one who wants to be an adult can ever be properly anorexic... In the end anorexia is not interesting enough to sustain an adult's attention.'

I thought I had broken free, because I so desperately wanted to be free; but now I can see that there are many ways of growing up, and that although I was always fiercely independent, this was a front, hiding my intense fears of the adult world. I had never really separated from my family, never accepted the necessary losses that come with growing up, and that this was why the 'old relics' could still come back to haunt me with such malignity.

I was lucky. There were always people around me who would listen to me endlessly repeating my litany of despair and who believed enough in me to continue telling me that life could and would get better. For my mother visiting me each and every day (I can still recall the sound of her shoes tripping along the corridor on the way to my room) it must have been so disheartening, watching me idling my life away in a hospital ward, complaining constantly about how much I was being made to eat, never a positive word to say about anything. But she did keep on coming. As did my friends. They must have wondered what good they were doing, but without their letters, cards, visits, persistence in keeping in touch, I would have been lost for ever.

Once, a dear friend from university arrived at the hospital. I was, of course, pleased to see her, but I was also so deeply ashamed of my state that I could not enjoy her visit. As is the cruel way with mental illness, it is often strangers and those less involved who end up saying and doing the things which have most impact. And the fact that her husband, whom I knew only slightly, had made the effort to come with her made a deeper impression; maybe I was not all bad.

For those closest to the anorexic, it is difficult. Whatever they do is unlikely to really get through those not-eating defences; they are just too much part of what has gone wrong. The key is to remain detached from the anorexic thoughts; to ignore the petty, deceitful behaviour, unless it impinges on other members of the family; and to avoid saying 'If you don't eat, you'll never get better.' Don't harp on about how happy, good, caring she used to be. Try to keep your own life going.

All impossible, when faced with a monosyllabic, negative response and an obstinate refusal to eat, especially when the point is reached that life itself is endangered. But the continual feeding of positive thoughts *will* make an impression. I can still remember the conversations when everything seemed to slip back into focus for a second before blurring over again. I don't remember what was said, just that feeling of connecting with something someone said and remembering what life could be like if eating was no longer a problem. One of the medical students, a bulky young man, told me he had once been anorexic. I couldn't believe it; he seemed so purposeful and athletic. But I was hugely moved by the fact that he could talk about it – and to me. Something in what he said got through – just a glimmer, but a glimmer nonetheless. And yet he will never have known that what he said had made an impression.

Each time this happened I got a little closer to recovery; a little closer to realising that it was up to me, and that only I could pick up that knife and fork and eat with resignation, if not relish. The message does eventually sink in: your life is worth living and eating just has to be part of that. It's the deal.

It's not that anorexics are uninterested in food; on the contrary, through constant denial they develop an unhealthy obsession with it. As they rush down the street in manic haste, they will often be seen to pause outside every baker's and confectioner's staring longingly at the window displays. They develop odd predilections for certain foods (just like pregnant women), which are always the same: raw vegetables and fruit (nothing tropical – too luxurious). Simone Weil wrote to her parents in August 1943 while she was in hospital and close to death: 'It will soon be harvest, and a splendid one they say. The strawberries are over. In their place one sees, first, "loganberries", a sort of wild raspberry with quite a raspberry taste but very rough and sometimes very tart; and then proper raspberries. Apart from fruit and pudding, the sweet course is nearly always with gelatine.' English puddings to a fastidious Frenchwoman must have been rather bizarre – all that wartime junket and dried-egg custard – but to know that she wrote this when she was so ill is also very strange.

When I was at home and not-eating, I used to have amazingly vivid dreams of bustling kitchens filled with huge trayloads of cakes, steak pies, vats of custard, apple tarts – steaming hot, fresh out of the oven, ready to take a bite. Then I would wake up with a start, creep downstairs (it was usually about three in the morning), take an apple out of the bowl, cut it in half, remove the core, slice one half into eight segments (leaving the other half in the fridge), eat each segment painfully slowly, before writing a note to my mother to confess how much I had eaten.

'Eating like a bird is considered feminine and appropriate and almost sanctified. Being able to withstand the temptation to indulge not only earns the admiration and envy of others, it increases one's own feelings of self-esteem. One has resisted where Eve didn't. One has refused the apple,' says Susie Orbach in *Hunger Strike*.

I can't say that I ever thought of myself as Eve – or that I ever knowingly refused an apple. All I knew was that I could not eat, and that I wanted somehow to purify myself. But then when hearing a line from a song by Natalie Merchant – 'Ever since Eden we're built for pleasing' – I found myself identifying immediately with what she was singing. Part of my rebellion (for that is what it was) was because I didn't want to please. Or, rather, I didn't want to please in the way that I thought was expected of me – because I feared that it would involve the suppression of all that I believed deep-down was real about me.

The anorexic has such a poor sense of who she is that she is unable to set the boundaries necessary for self-preservation. She is terrified of close relationships because she fears she will be overwhelmed, unable to breathe, flattened and denied her personality. These fears will not go away until she has acquired enough confidence and self-awareness to allow someone in without any sense of loss. This is why she is reluctant to take on the adult world, with all that this means.

An article in the *Journal of Criminal Psychopathology* for January 1942 attempted to explain this rather differently. Its author, P. Lionel Goitein, argued that the anorexic is in fact a potential prostitute: she deprives herself of food to ensure that she does not become promiscuous:

Anorexia nervosa is a well recognised clinical entity characterised by an ever-increasing disinclination and disability to take solid food (and sometimes fluids also) with loss of weight and of zest, loss of relish and sexual appetency and resulting in inertia and exhaustion, malaise and symptoms of hypochondria, occurring in young women of a special class: viz of leptosomatic and somewhat asthenic build, with tendency to hirsuteness and amenorrhoea, flat chest and small breasts; infantile, attractive baby-faced, of fine proportions and of good carriage, hysterically exhibitionistic and seductive but with an incapacity for real love relationship, i.e., the potential prostitute.

It's the 'i.e.' that is extraordinary. And his explanation for such behaviour is even more so:

They are prepared to be treated as toys, dancing partners and models or interesting specimens. They often drink and smoke to excess and have occasional bouts of secret feeding, but for the most part succeed in becoming only 'interesting invalids', wasted to a shadow and wilting as a flower, with a thoroughly inordinate craving for sympathy.

Goitein based his conclusions on several prostitutes whom he had treated who were anorexic and alcoholic. He admitted that he had used 'minimal data' and that his paper was 'an aspect of the subject offered as a footnote to the problem not usually noted'. Well there's a relief. It's only a 'footnote' – and I only quote it here to show how much misunderstanding there was, and still is, about what causes anorexia. Because, of course, there is a much simpler explanation for the anorexic's ambivalence about sex. To be sexual is to be adult, to take risks, to make compromises, to take responsibility for your destiny, your life; something that the anorexic is rejecting through her rejection of food. And just as she is terrified of her appetite for food, in case it gets out of control, so she is terrified of any surges of desire. That's it, really. That's all that needs to be understood, although it has taken me 20-odd years to be able to acknowledge this; and to accept that one's feelings, thoughts, emotions can be contradictory, that no one thing is true.

How do you know when an anorexic has got over her illness? I asked Gill Todd at the Hope Seminar. 'When she can form an individual relationship,' she replied. I was not quite sure what she meant, until Monty Don told me, 'The secret of overcoming anorexia is to feel sufficiently loved and looked after that you can surrender to it; that is the key – letting go.' It's resolving not to resolve; it's allowing someone else into your life, for whom you are responsible, and whom you allow to be responsible for you. Once you do that, all sorts of things become possible. Having accepted that someone can love you, really love you as you are, then you have to begin to love yourself. If you can love yourself, even your not-so-lovable body, then not-eating becomes an irrelevant response.

The other day I had lunch with my parents to celebrate Dad's birthday. It was a lovely sunny April day. We walked along the river and sat in a dining-room with windows overlooking the water. The setting was perfect, the atmosphere less hectic than usual in a City restaurant, the menu less complicated: a set lunch of two courses at a remarkably reasonable price or à la carte. We chose the former: all three of us. Gravadlax followed by roast guinea fowl (meat!). It was so obvious. The usual drama over choosing what I should eat no longer seemed relevant. My mother looked at me in amazement. And as we ate – with relish – I could see her amazement turning into quiet relief; and I could feel within me that something had changed; another cog had turned.

In looking again at what I put myself and my family through all those years ago, I have at last realised that I don't need to feel ashamed of it. It was something that happened, just like any other illness. And it's not all bad – though most of it is. I would not wish anorexia on anyone, but I know that without it I would not be the person I am now. Maybe I have been shown to be vulnerable; maybe I was unable to look at the realities of life without flinching. But having been forced to look at the darkness within – and survived – I need never be frightened again. Nor need you. That's the key: to be able to look through a glass, darkly and not care.

RECOMMENDED READING

ARMSTRONG, Karen: *Beginning the World* (Macmillan, 1983). An autobiographical account of her descent into anorexia on leaving convent life. Very realistic.

BRUCH, Hilde: *Eating Disorders: Obesity, Anorexia Nervosa and the Person Within* (Routledge, 1974). A revelatory view of the condition by a consultant psychiatrist who believes that depression precedes not-eating.

BRUCH, Hilde: *The Golden Cage: The Enigma of Anorexia Nervosa* (Open Books, 1978). A much more conversational account, with lots of personal stories.

BRUCH, Hilde (edited by Danita Czyzewski and Melanie A. Suhr): *Conversations with Anorexics* (Basic Books, 1988). A posthumous edition of tapes made by Bruch during her sessions with anorexics and their families.

DON, Monty: 'How I Grew Up and Filled Out', *Sunday Telegraph Review* (11 February 1996). Frank account of anorexia from the male point of view.

GRAY, Francine du Plessix: *Simone Weil* (Weidenfeld & Nicolson, 2001). The influential French philosopher died, aged 34, from complications brought on by her not-eating habits.

GROSS, Philip: *The Wasting Game* (Bloodaxe, 1998). A collection of poems written from the point of view of a father of a teenage anorexic.

HAMSUN, Knut (translated by Sverre Lyngstad): *Hunger*

(Rebel Inc., 1996). Startling descriptions of what it is like to go without food.

KAFKA, Franz: 'The Hunger Artist', in *The Complete Stories* (edited by Nahum N. Glatzer with a foreword by John Updike, Schocken, 1995). Tellingly satirical account of what it is to go on hunger strike.

MacLEOD, Sheila: *The Art of Starvation: One Girl's Journey through Adolescence and Anorexia – A Story of Survival* (Virago, 1981). The author is convinced that there are strong links between the illness and the cultural expectations placed on women.

MANTEL, Hilary: *An Experiment in Love* (Viking, 1995). At one point the female narrator says that this is not an anorexic novel – but she is.

MARGOLIS, Karen: *To Eat or Not to Eat* (Camden Press, 1988). A sort of West Coast America account of anorexia by an older woman.

MILLER, Alice: *The Drama of Being a Child: The Search for the True Self* (revised edition, Virago, 2001). Not about anorexia, but fascinating insights into the way children fail to develop the good self-esteem essential to harmonious adulthood.

PALAZZOLI, Mara Selvini: *Self-Starvation: From Individual to Family Therapy in the Treatment of Anorexia Nervosa* (Jason Aronson Inc., 1996). A startlingly brutal description of the disease and how it affects the behaviour of those who suffer from it. She began by treating anorexics individually but now views the illness as being very much about family dynamics that go wrong.

RHYS, Jean: 'Hunger' from *The Left Bank and Other Stories* (Jonathan Cape, 1927). Powerful description of starvation's endorphinous highs and lows.

TODD, Gill, WHITAKER, Wendy and GAVAN, Kay: 'Eating Disorders', *Mental Illness: A Handbook for Carers*, edited by Rosalind Ramsay, Claire Gerada, Sarah Mars and George Szmukler (Jessica Kingsley Publishers, 2001). This chapter by the nursing team at the Bethlem Royal Hospital in Surrey contains both illuminating case-studies and advice.

WEIL, Simone: *Seventy Letters*, translated and arranged by Richard Rees (Oxford University Press, 1965). In these letters to family, friends and colleagues, Weil's extraordinary intelligence and personality shine through.

REFERENCES

BELL, Rudolph M.: *Holy Anorexia* (University of Chicago Press, 1985). Rather far-fetched comparisons between modern anorexia and the cult of fasting among medieval saints such as St Catherine of Siena.

BRUMBERG, Joan Jacobs: *Fasting Girls: The Emergence of Anorexia Nervosa as a Modern Disease* (Harvard University Press, 1988). An historical analysis of the condition from the fasting saints to celebrity tragedies such as Karen Carpenter via the Victorian vegetarians and Edwardian suffragettes.

CLAUDE-PIERRE, Peggy: *The Secret Language of Eating Disorders: The Revolutionary New Approach to Understanding and Curing Anorexia Nervosa* (Bantam, 1998). A Canadian mother (turned counsellor) of anorexic daughters recounts her experiences. Lots of hugging – and tears – but with insights too.

CRISP, A.H.: *Anorexia Nervosa: The Wish to Change, Self-Help and Discovery – The Thirty Steps* (Psychology Press, 1996). A self-help book written by one of Britain's experts on anorexia.

DALLY, Peter: *Anorexia Nervosa* (William Heinemann, 1969). Dally was one of the leading psychiatrists dealing with anorexia in the 1960s and 1970s.

DALLY, Peter and GOMEZ, Jean: *Understanding Anorexia Nervosa and Obesity: A Sense of Proportion* (Faber, 1990). Some 20 years later, Dally revises his views on treatment.

ELLMANN, Maud: *The Hunger Artists: Starving, Writing and Imprisonment* (Virago, 1993). Vivid account, linking the Irish hunger-strikers with women anorexics.

GEE, Samuel: *Medical Lectures and Aphorisms* (Hodder & Stoughton, 1915). Quotes from Thomas Hobbes's letter of 1688.

GULL, Sir William Withey: 'Anorexia Nervosa (Apepsia Hysterica, Anorexia Hysterica)', *Transactions of the Clinical Society*, 7 (London, 1874). The first exposition of anorexia nervosa in English, illustrated with before-and-after engravings.

GULL, Sir William Withey: 'Anorexia Nervosa', *The Lancet*, 17 March 1888. Case-history with illustrations, which provokes an editorial comment in the following week's edition.

LASEGUE, Charles: 'On Hysterical Anorexia' (translated from the *Archives Générales de Médecine*, April 1873), *The Medical Times and Gazette*, 2 (London 1873). The French physician pre-empted Sir William Gull in naming the condition.

LAWRENCE, Marilyn: *The Anorexic Experience* (The Women's Press, 1984). An attempt to label anorexia as a feminist illness.

LEMMA-WRIGHT, Alessandra: *Starving to Live: The Paradox of Anorexia Nervosa* (Central Book Publishing,

1994). A clinical psychologist explains the contradictory nature of the illness.

LINDSAY, Clare: *Conquering Anorexia: The Route to Recovery* (Summersdale, 2000). Clare, a teenage anorexic, was a day patient in an NHS counselling and psychotherapy unit. Her solution: 'necessary selfishness'.

Living with a Hijacker: Personal Stories Presented by Sufferers, jointly produced by the Eating Disorders Association and Bethlem Royal Hospital, South London and Maudsley NHS Trust (June 2001).

LOCK, James, LE GRANGE, Daniel, AGRAS, W. Stewart and DARE, Christopher (eds): *Treatment Manual for Anorexia Nervosa: A Family-Based Approach* (The Guilford Press, 2000). An explanation of the methods used at the Maudsley Hospital in south London, working with anorexics and their families.

MacSWEEN, Morag: *Anorexic Bodies: A Feminist and Sociological Perspective on Anorexia Nervosa* (Routledge, 1993), Another attempt to categorise anorexia as a cultural illness.

MAXTED, Anna: *Running in Heels* (Arrow, 2001). A schlocky blockbuster novel by a recovered anorexic.

MORTON, Richard: *Phthisiologia; or, a Treatise of Consumptions* (translated from the original 1689 Latin edition, London, 1694). The first (or so it is claimed) description of the condition by an expert on consumptive illnesses.

ORBACH, Susie: *Hunger Strike: The Anorectic's Struggle*

as a Metaphor for our Age (Faber, 1986). Orbach's follow-up to her enormously influential *Fat Is a Feminist Issue.*

ORBACH, Susie: *On Eating* (Penguin, 2002). A self-help manual.

REYNOLDS, John: *A Discourse Upon Prodigious Abstinence, Occasioned by the Twelve Months Fasting of Martha Taylor, The Famed Derbyshire Damosell...* (Printed by R.W. for Nevill Simmons, at the Sign of the Three Crowns near Holborn..., 1669). Reynolds argues that prolonged fasting is not miraculous but is possible physiologically.

SMITH, Joan: *Hungry for You: Essays and Extracts* (Chatto & Windus, 1986). Literary allusions to hunger strikes and attitudes to eating.

WOLF, Naomi: *The Beauty Myth: How Images of Female Beauty Are Used Against Women* (William Morrow, 1991).

Advice and Treatment

Breathe and Relax: A Way to Healing: an 80-minute audio cassette containing simple breathing, meditation and relaxation techniques. Available (UK only) for £7.50 including postage from Julie Friedeberger, 16 Coleraine Road, London SE3 7PQ

Eating Disorders Association
First Floor, Wensum House, 103 Prince of Wales Road, Norwich NR1 1DW
Helpline: 0845 6341414 (Mon to Fri, 8.30am to 8.30pm)
Youthline: 0845 6347650 (Mon to Fri, 4pm to 6.30pm)

Newmarket House Clinic
153 Newmarket Road, Norwich NR4 6SY. Tel: 01603 452226

AUTHOR BIOGRAPHY

Kate Chisholm grew up in London. She studied history at
Edinburgh University and now works as a literary journal-
ist. She reviews regularly for the *Sunday Telegraph*, the
Evening Standard, the *Daily Mail* and the BBC History
Magazine. Her first book, *Fanny Burney: Her Life*, was
published by Chatto & Windus in 1998.